Modern Automotive HVAC Systems

BOOK 1

Mechanical Systems
Operation and Design
including Fundamentals,
Service, Diagnostics
and Repair

For more information, contact:

MACS Worldwide™
P.O. Box 88
225 S. Broad Street
Lansdale, Pa, 19446
Voice: 215-631-7020
Fax: 215-631-7017
E-mail: info@macsw.org

MACS® and the MACS® logo are registered trademarks of
the Mobile Air Conditioning Society Worldwide™
All Rights Reserved. Printed in the U.S.A.

© 2011, © 2016, Mobile Air Conditioning Society Worldwide™

TABLE OF CONTENTS

Introduction

PREFACE:

Welcome! This book is aimed at a broad section of automotive repair professionals including students, entry-level technicians, and the seasoned professional. It is designed to educate, develop and maintain professional level skills to make you efficient and effective in your shop.

Automotive climate control has evolved quickly in the past 30 years; air conditioning was once a luxury option but has become standard today on almost every vehicle. Additionally, mainly due to environmental concerns, climate control is one of the very few systems on a vehicle governed by specific rules and laws for material handling and technician certification.

Today's technician must be more than a parts-changer. As HVAC systems become more sophisticated and incorporate extensive computer controls, more sensors, new components and new refrigerants, old knowledge will no longer serve.

To be successful at any level of repair, a technician must understand many things and be able to use that knowledge every day. Safety is paramount—A/C systems operate under pressure, components and fluids can be very hot or cold, and compressed refrigerant gas or lubricants can cause injury as well as mechanical damage. What you don't do can hurt you.

Successful troubleshooting requires your knowledge of the basic principles shared by all systems, the specific components and controls used on the car in the bay, and the proper operation of shop service and diagnostic tools. A scan tool may show you a stored code or DTC but it won't find a pinhole leak in a refrigerant line.

The shop and its staff must also work within environmental guidelines or risk stiff fines from authorities. New refrigerants, chemicals and components will only add to the required level of knowledge and technicians will be challenged to keep their own knowledge – and their equipment – current.

Now it's all up to you. This book is designed to sharpen your skills through both a review of basic principles and presentation of industry-accepted best practices for all aspects of HVAC diagnosis and repair.

Your customers expect you to do the right thing and follow correct procedures. Shortcuts are rarely satisfactory—work safely, and always use the correct equipment. It's what makes you a professional.

NOTES:

NOTES:

SAFETY AND PRECAUTIONS

- In a good system, refrigerant lines are always under pressure and should only be disconnected after the refrigerant charge has been recovered.

- Always wear eye protection and cotton-lined barrier gloves while servicing air conditioning systems or handling refrigerant.

- Refrigerant will evaporate quickly at atmospheric pressure and will freeze skin and eye tissue. Serious injury or blindness could result if contact is made with liquid refrigerant.

- Avoid breathing refrigerant or refrigerant oil vapor. Exposure may irritate eyes, nose, and throat. If contact is made, seek immediate medical attention.

- Do not expose refrigerant to an open flame or extremely hot surfaces such as exhaust components. Decomposition of the refrigerant creates hazardous substances.

- R-134a air conditioning systems should not be pressure-tested or leak-tested with compressed air. Combustible mixtures of air and R-134a may form, resulting in fire or explosion.

- Refrigerant released in a closed area will displace oxygen and cause suffocation. Work in an area where there is a constant flow of fresh air when a system is recovered, charged, and leak-tested.

- Never expose refrigerant containers to temperatures over 125° F (52° C). Exceeding this temperature may cause the container to explode.

- Use only recovery, recycle, and recharge equipment that meets SAE J2210 or J2788 certification.

- Refrigerant oil absorbs moisture. Do not open a container of refrigerant oil until you are ready to use it. Replace the cap on the oil container immediately after use.

- Refrigerant oil can damage paint, plastic parts, drive belts and coolant hoses. Use caution to prevent refrigerant oil from contacting these items.

- Use only the refrigerant recommended for the vehicle's system.

- Use only the refrigerant oil that is recommended for the system on the vehicle.

- Observe all warnings to avoid the risk of personal injury.

- Observe all cautions to avoid damage to service equipment and the vehicle.

- Never reuse O-rings or gaskets; tighten refrigerant fittings and components to the correct torque value.

- Use a backup wrench to prevent twisting of the refrigerant lines or tubes.

GOING GREEN

The automotive repair industry has been in the forefront of environmental issues beginning back in the early 1960s when the PCV valve was mandated. As the decades rolled on, more emission control components were added and more regulations were implemented.

In 1974, chlorine based (CFC) refrigerants were tied to environmental concerns with regard to ozone depletion. In 1987, steps were taken to phase out ozone-depleting substances including R-12 refrigerant used in mobile air conditioning systems. By 1995, the production of R-12 refrigerant in the United States ended and the switch to R-134a (which began in 1992) was completed on new production vehicles.

Increased concerns about the global warming potential of R-134a lead the European Union to ban the use of R-134a in mobile air conditioning systems beginning with new models in 2011.

These global concerns regarding the release of refrigerants during the service of mobile A/C systems has resulted in revised standards for service procedures and equipment. To reduce refrigerant emissions during service, new equipment and servicing procedures have been developed. Additionally, improved system designs will result in reduced refrigerant emissions and increased system operating efficiencies.

Notes:

Section 1: Principles of Operation

HOW AIR CONDITIONING WORKS

Heat enters a vehicle in many ways; from the sun, from the road surface, and from the working parts of the vehicle itself. The purpose of air conditioning is to remove heat from the passenger compartment and release it to the outside air. This is accomplished through the controlled evaporation and condensation of a chemical substance. The chemical substance for current mobile A/C systems is refrigerant R-134a.

The HVAC systems use the principles of heat transfer, pressure, condensation and evaporation to remove heat from the passenger compartment.

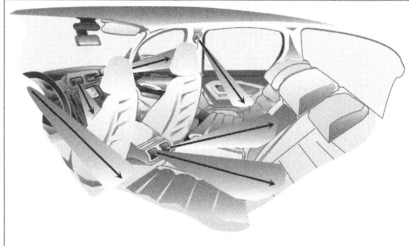

What is Air Conditioning?

Operating Principles

- For the system to work, refrigerant must be able to change quickly from a liquid to a gas and back again. The current refrigerant R-134a, and its predecessor R-12, both had that ability, as does the new R-1234yf which will be introduced in some vehicles starting in 2012.

- Heat always moves from a warmer area to a colder area. This is a basic law of physics.

- As the refrigerants change from a liquid to a gas **(evaporation)**, large amounts of heat will be absorbed.

- As the refrigerants change from a gas to a liquid **(condensation)**, large amounts of heat will be released.

Evaporation and condensation are the key words. Evaporation occurs in the evaporator core, the heat exchanger located near the passenger compartment which absorbs heat. Condensation occurs in the condenser, the heat exchanger which releases the

Condenser   **Evaporator**

Condenser and Evaporator

heat to the outside air. It is located near the radiator in front of the vehicle.

Pressure Temperature Relationship

How a particular substance responds when it is pressurized, heated or cooled can be calculated. For example water at atmospheric pressure (14.7 psi) will boil at 212°F. When the pressure is reduced, liquids boil at a lower temperature. For example, under a vacuum of 29.5 inches Hg, water will boil at 53° F.

R-134a Pressure/Temperature Relationship

Degrees (F)	PSI (Gauge)	Degrees (F)	PSI (Gauge)
15	15	110	146
20	18	115	158
25	22	120	171
30	26	125	185
35	30	130	198
40	35	135	212
45	40	140	228
50	45	145	244
55	51	150	262
60	57	155	280
65	64	160	299
70	71	165	319
75	79	170	339
80	87	175	361
85	95	180	384
90	104	185	408
95	114	190	433
100	124	195	459
105	135	200	486

Notes:

Notes:

The pressure of refrigerant varies with temperature and the temperature of the refrigerant varies with the amount of pressure applied. These pressure/temperature changes are measurable, and charts have been developed to provide specific pressure at a given temperature to aid in diagnosing the A/C system.

Heat Transfer

An understanding of types of heat transfer is helpful when diagnosing an A/C system.

Convection occurs when heat is transferred by the flow of a liquid. An example would be coolant flowing through the heater core. When the vehicle blower moves heated air into the passenger compartment, the heat is being transferred by convection.

Conduction occurs when heat is transferred by two objects touching each other. If a piece of hot metal is placed against cold metal, the heat will travel from the hot metal to the cold metal through conduction. A thermal shield may be placed around A/C components to prevent an additional heat load being added to the A/C system through the conduction process.

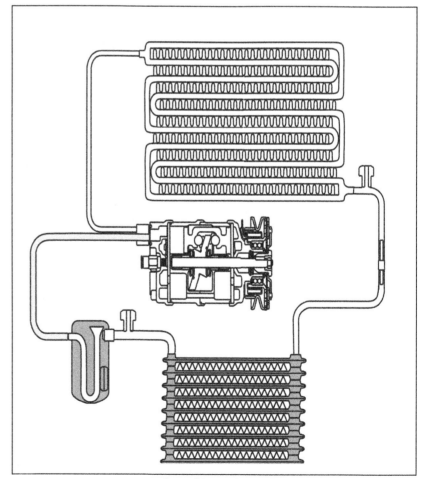

The Refrigeration Cycle

Radiation occurs when heat energy is transferred using a different energy source. When the sun shines through the glass into a vehicle, the energy of the light is transformed into heat. For example, vehicle paint and interior color can affect system performance.

The Refrigeration Cycle

The A/C system is a closed, pressurized system; components include: a compressor, condenser, filter drier device, metering device, evaporator and plumbing consisting of rubber hoses and metal pipes connecting the pieces together. The A/C system is divided into two sides; high-pressure and low-pressure. The dividing points in the system are the compressor and the metering device. The high-pressure side is divided into hot, high-pressure gas and warm, high-pressure liquid. The low-pressure side is divided into cool, low-pressure liquefied gas and cold, low-pressure gas. The next section will cover A/C system types and components.

Notes:

Section 2: System Designs and Components

Notes:

A/C SYSTEM DESIGNS

The two most common A/C system designs are shown below. In the Thermostatic Expansion Valve/Receiver Drier design (TXV/RD), the receiver/drier is the main filter.

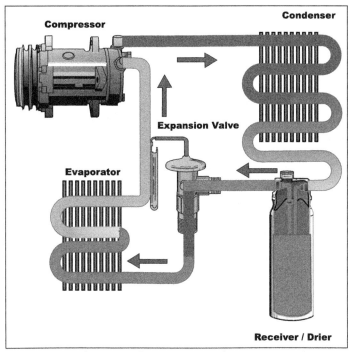

Thermostatic Expansion Valve System

In the Orifice Tube/Accumulator (OT) design, the orifice tube is the main filter of the system.

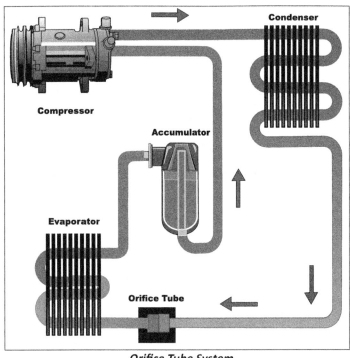

Orifice Tube System

Regardless of system design, A/C system operation is based on the constant interaction between the compressor and the metering device, either a TXV or an OT. In an operating A/C system, the low-pressure refrigerant vapor is drawn into the compressor, compressed and becomes a hot, high-pressure vapor. The hot, high-pressure vapor travels through the discharge line into the inlet of the condenser, where the refrigerant vapor transfers the latent heat to the condenser passages and fins. As the refrigerant vapor releases the heat, it condenses into a high-pressure liquid.

If the system metering device is a TXV, the high-pressure liquid enters the top of the receiver drier. The receiver drier contains a desiccant material that will absorb moisture that has entered the system. The receiver drier will also have a filter screen to trap debris. The high-pressure liquid refrigerant travels through the liquid line to the TXV. As the high-pressure refrigerant passes through an orifice inside the TXV, its pressure drops.

Entering the evaporator core as a low-pressure liquefied gas, its temperature drops and the refrigerant begins to absorb heat from the air that is passing through the fins of the evaporator core. The low-pressure low temperature refrigerant vapor leaves the evaporator through the suction line and returns to the compressor to begin the process over again.

In an orifice tube system, the orifice tube provides a restriction to the high-pressure liquid refrigerant as it leaves the condenser, reducing its pressure as it meters refrigerant into the evaporator as a low-pressure liquefied gas. Located in the refrigerant line between the condenser outlet and the evaporator inlet, the orifice tube separates the high-pressure side from the low-pressure side of the A/C system.

The refrigerant flow rate through the orifice is determined by the diameter of the metal tube inside the orifice tube's plastic housing. The opening can either be fixed or variable depending on the system manufacturer, but is usually fixed. The orifice tube contains a filter screen that is the main filter of the system.

Orifice tube systems do not meter refrigerant flow based on temperature. This makes it possible for refrigerant to pass through the evaporator as a liquid. If liquid enters the compressor damage can occur, because a compressor is designed to pump vapor only. To prevent liquid refrigerant from reaching the compressor, a device called the accumulator is located between the outlet of the evaporator and the compressor.

Notes:

It is a liquid-vapor separator which will allow only vapor to reach the compressor inlet. The accumulator also contains a desiccant to remove moisture from the system.

Both system designs contain additional switches and controls to maintain evaporator core temperature to prevent freeze up, and protection devices to prevent system damage caused by excessively high or low-pressures and temperatures. These systems and devices will be covered in detail in another section.

SYSTEM COMPONENTS FOUND ON BOTH DESIGNS

Compressors

The compressor is the heart of the A/C system, a pump that is, in most systems, belt driven by the engine. Its job is to pump the refrigerant through the A/C system and to increase its pressure. Increasing the refrigerant pressure increases its temperature. This ensures complete heat transfer in the condenser. The compressor is one of the two dividing points between the low-pressure and high-pressure sides of the A/C system. The low-pressure refrigerant vapor is drawn into the suction side of the compressor. The compressor will use pistons, vanes, or a scroll to compress the refrigerant vapor. The compressed refrigerant travels out of the compressor and through the discharge line towards the condenser. A small amount of compressor oil also circulates through the system. Compressors, like people, come in all shapes and sizes.

FIXED DISPLACEMENT COMPRESSORS

A fixed displacement compressor's output is dependent on the speed of the engine. To control the flow and to meet the demands of the refrigeration system, the compressor is cycled off and on.

Fixed displacement compressors can be either piston, vane, or scroll design. These compressors differ in design and displacement, but compress the same amount of refrigerant with each rotation. Most are controlled by cycling off and on according to the pressure or temperature on the low-pressure side of the system. The compressor is mounted on the engine, and most have an electromagnetic clutch that is belt driven by the engine. When the compressor is cycled on, the compressor clutch is energized and the engine turns the compressor crankshaft. When the compressor cycles off, the clutch drive hub is de-energized, and the pulley on the compressor turns with the drive belt.

Compressor

Fixed Displacement Compressor

Piston Compressors

The piston compressor driveshaft moves the compressor pistons back and forth. The movement of the pistons draws in the refrigerant on the low side and pumps it out on the high side. On the suction stroke the piston moves rearward in the cylinder, creating an area of low-pressure in the cylinder that seats the discharge reed valve and opens the suction reed. This low-pressure draws in the refrigerant vapor. The compression stroke moves the piston forward in the cylinder and compresses the refrigerant vapor. The pressure developed by the compression opens the discharge reed valve forcing the high-pressure refrigerant vapor into the discharge line. The suction port is usually marked with the letter "S" and the discharge side with the letter "D." Another way to determine which port is the suction or discharge, is that the diameter of the suction port will be larger than the diameter of the discharge port. There are various piston compressor designs. They are all similar in operation, but there are some significant differences.

Piston Compressor

Swash Plate Compressors

These types of compressors usually contain six or ten cylinders. The dual-sided pistons in an opposed axial compressor consist of a one-piece casting. A rotating device called the swash plate causes the pistons to move. The swash plate is an elliptical disc that is mounted at an angle to the compressor drive shaft. The rotation of the swash plate moves the pistons parallel to the drive shaft. Another component, called a slipper disc, slides on the swash plate, and a ball rides in a socket in the slipper disc. The ball also rides in a socket in the piston, in effect connecting the piston and slipper disc.

Swash Plate Compressor Components

Wobble Plate Compressors

The single row axial compressor has five, six or seven pistons connected to a wobble plate. The pistons' connecting rods have a ball mounted on each end, and these balls fit into sockets on each piston and on the wobble plate. The wobble plate is held in place by anti-rotation gears. A cam rotor behind the wobble plate causes it to rotate. The combination of the rotating cam and the stationary wobble plate causes the pistons to move in a plane parallel to the compressor drive shaft.

FIXED DISPLACEMENT COMPRESSOR VARIATIONS

Besides piston type, fixed displacement compressors, and compressors that use vanes and scrolls, are found on many vehicle models. The advantages to these designs are less weight and smaller size as well as quieter and more efficient operation.

Wobble Plate Compressor

Rotary Vane Compressor

Rotary Vane Compressor – Impeller

Scroll Compressor

Vane Compressors

Rotary vane compressors contain a solid rotating cylinder called an impeller. The impeller is equipped with vanes that move in and out of slots in the impeller. The impeller is placed within an elliptically shaped chamber containing a large volume section and a small volume section. Low-pressure/low temperature refrigerant vapor is drawn into the large volume section. The vane's sweeping motion forces the refrigerant vapor into the small volume section, compressing it, and causing it to change into high-pressure/high temperature vapor. Some vane compressors are equipped with a control valve to automatically vary its output as the system heat loads change.

Scroll Compressors

Scroll compressors contain two scroll-shaped elements. One is fixed (non-moveable), and is part of the compressor case or housing. The other is a moveable scroll which orbits inside the fixed scroll. An eccentric on the compressor's driveshaft gives motion to the moveable scroll.

As the moveable scroll orbits inside the fixed scroll, low-pressure/low temperature refrigerant vapor is drawn into the compressor. The refrigerant vapor is compressed toward the center of the fixed scroll, where it is forced out the discharge valve as a high temperature/high-pressure vapor, to the condenser. The scroll compressor has a longer compression cycle. This minimizes torque fluctuation and vibration. Some scroll compressors' capacities change with cooling load. This feature minimizes clutch cycling and engine speed changes. The compressor capacity is regulated with a bypass valve and a control valve. The control valve senses the pressure on the low side of the system.

Scroll Compressor - Internal View

VARIABLE DISPLACEMENT COMPRESSORS

Variable displacement compressors are usually 5, 6, or 7 cylinder wobble plate designs. Unlike fixed displacement compressors, the amount of refrigerant they pump can vary. This is accomplished by changing the stroke of their pistons. Because refrigerant flow, so subsequently, evaporator temperature, are controlled by the compressor changing displacement, there is no need for to their clutches to cycle. So cycling switches and their associated circuitry can be eliminated.

Displacement is controlled by changes in internal crankcase pressure. Crankcase pressure is controlled through the operation of a control valve. The control valve is mounted in a passage in the rear of the compressor. Two types of control valves are used. One type is a mechanical valve; the other an electronically controlled solenoid.

Variable displacement compressors provide for very smooth operation, eliminating the "thumps" sometimes felt as compressor clutches engage and disengage. Also eliminated is the annoyance of engine rpm rising and falling, as is sometimes experienced with a conventional compressor as the clutch engages and disengages. Variable displacement piston compressors also help improve fuel economy.

Variable Displacement Compressor

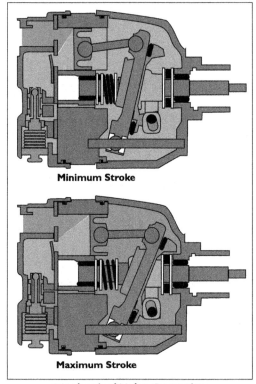

Minimum Stroke

Maximum Stroke

Mechanical Valve Operation

Variable Displacement Compressor Design and Operation

While designs vary, the following provides a general description concerning how most of these special compressors are constructed.

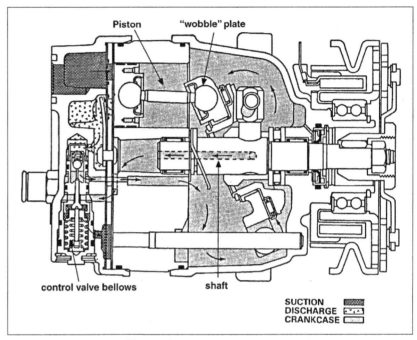

Variable Displacement Compressor Design

Bearings on each end of the compressor case support the wobble plate's drive shaft. Another part, called a drive plate, is connected to the driveshaft with a swivel joint made up of a drive lug. A guide pin fits into an eccentric slot in the drive lug. The drive lug serves as the connection between the driveshaft and drive plate. Because of this, as the driveshaft turns, it also causes the drive plate to turn.

A needle bearing assembly is between the drive plate and the wobble plate. When the wobble plate and drive plate are both canted to an angle with the driveshaft, the spinning of the driveshaft through a cam-type socket joint causes the drive and wobble plate to wobble. As this occurs, the pistons, which are connected to the wobble plate by connecting rods, reciprocate in their cylinders.

When the wobble plate is tilted all the way back, it's not at much of an angle; as a matter of fact, barely any angle at all. So even when the driveshaft is spinning, the wobble plate barely wobbles, and there is very little piston movement. However, even with the wobble plate tilted back as far as it can go, there will always be some movement of the wobble plate, and subsequently, some reciprocation of the pistons.

How the Control Valve Works

The control valve contains a thermostatic pressure-sensitive bellows which is exposed to suction side pressure. The bellows acts on a ball and pin valve which is exposed to high side pressure. The bellows also controls a bleed port that is exposed to suction side pressure.

For increased stroke and displacement, pressure inside the crankcase is reduced, so the opposing force on the pistons causes the wobble plate to tilt to a greater angle. When reduced stroke (and therefore displacement and compressor output) is called for, pressure in the crankcase is increased. This results in an increase in pressure behind the pistons, so the angle of the wobble plate becomes less severe, reducing piston displacement and compressor output.

When low side pressure is above approximately 30 psi, increased cooling is needed, so displacement must increase. Higher low side pressure causes bellows in the control valve to contract. When the bellows contract, the pin inside the control valve drops and a spring, as well as high-side pressure, pushes the ball against the seat in a high-side passage, closing it. This blocks high-side pressure from entering the crankcase. Simultaneously, the bleed port from the suction side to the crankcase opens, and some crankcase pressure enters the suction side. This causes a reduction in crankcase pressure. The opposing force behind the pistons causes the wobble plate to tilt for increased displacement.

When low side pressure drops below approximately 30 psi, the control valve bellows expands and pushes the ball off its seat. High side pressure flows through the control valve assembly into the crankcase. This results in an increase in crankcase pressure against the spring on the crankshaft and on the back side of the pistons. This moves the wobble plate to a reduced angle and also reduces piston stroke and displacement.

The control valve is continuously modulating, so under conditions of moderate cooling demand, the displacement of the compressor will remain somewhere around mid-stroke. Obviously, under conditions of low cooling demand, the displacement of the compressor will stay toward the low end. Conversely, under conditions of high cooling demand, the displacement of the compressor will stay toward the high end.

Control Valve

NOTES

CLUTCHLESS VARIABLE DISPLACEMENT COMPRESSORS

Some of the most modern variable displacement compressors do not have a clutch. In these compressors, instead of a mechanical bellows-type control valve, an electrically operated solenoid-type control valve is used. The solenoids are controlled by a microprocessor for precise regulation according to signals from temperature sensors and other inputs.

Because there is no clutch, there is no way to turn these types of compressor on or off. Cold weather or hot, or anywhere in between, the compressor pulley should always be spinning – unless there's a failure, which will be explained at the end of this section.

How Clutchless Variable Compressors Work

The solenoid valve controls a passage between the discharge (high pressure) and suction (low pressure) sides. The suction side and the crankcase are also connected by a restricted passage. When the solenoid valve is closed, the pressures between the crankcase and cylinders are balanced, and the wobble plate is maintained in a nearly level position by a coil spring, so any pumping is the minimum. As the solenoid valve opens under computer command, the pressures between the crankcase and cylinders become unbalanced – more pressure in the cylinders than in the crankcase. So the pressure "above" the pistons pushes back, tilting the wobble plate back for increased piston stroke and more pumping action. The more the solenoid opens, the greater the wobble plate tilt and pumping action. As the solenoid valve closes, the reverse occurs – less pressure in the cylinders, and the combination of crankcase pressure and spring pressure tilts the wobble plate in the opposite direction, toward a more level position.

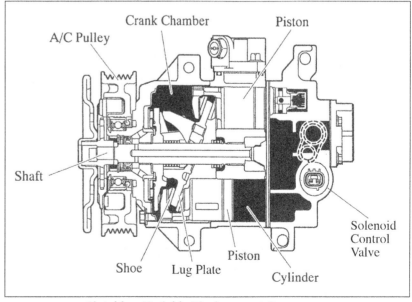

Clutchless Variable Displacement Compressor

The solenoid's electronic controller makes the decisions whether to increase or decrease the duty cycle of the solenoid valve. The lower the duty cycle, the less open the solenoid valve and the smaller the compressor displacement. The higher the duty cycle, the greater the displacement.

At the computer end, the cooling load (how much A/C is needed) is calculated, and solenoid/compressor operation is commanded to provide it, based on readings from a number of sensors. There may be an evaporator temperature sensor, but it provides just one piece of information, as the evaporator temperature is not reduced to 32 degrees F. then reheated, as in a conventional compressor system. In this design, the evaporator temperature is allowed to be whatever is appropriate for the cooling load – even into the 40s and 50s F. This produces a much greater energy saving than cooling and then reheating to provide the motorist's selected comfort level.

Clutchless Compressor Control Valve

Sensors and inputs that may be used include:

- Ambient air temperature sensor
- In-car temperature sensor
- Evaporator temperature sensor
- Engine coolant temperature sensor
- Sunload sensor
- Refrigerant pressure sensor (high-side transducer)
- Control panel temperature knob
- Fan speed switch position (low vs. high), and whether or not the system is in outside air or recirc.

Compressor Pulley Not Spinning?

In case of compressor seizure, to protect the drive belt (which may operate other engine-driven accessories), the pulley/hub assembly is designed to separate, so the pulley can keep spinning and the other belt-driven accessories (power steering, water pump, alternator) can also keep operating.

Notes:

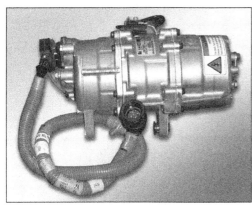

Electric Compressor

Notes:

ELECTRIC COMPRESSORS

There is currently an increase in the number of hybrid vehicles that are equipped with an electrically driven compressor. Before this, most hybrids were equipped with belt driven compressors that required engine operation to provide cooling.

In 2004, some hybrids began to use a brushless electric motor to run the compressor. The compressors are scroll designs with built-in oil separators which keep most of the oil inside the compressor. The compressors are equipped with an AC inverter that converts the high-voltage battery's DC voltage to AC voltage needed to operate the compressor. Depending on the year and model of the vehicle, the AC inverter will be a separate module, or built into the compressor.

The motors on these compressors require between 144 volts and 300 volts, depending on the manufacturer and vehicle model.

Electrically driven compressors use a very specific Polyolester (POE) oil and it cannot be interchanged with Polyalkylene Glycol (PAG) oil or regular ester oil.

Hybrid vehicles must be handled carefully. Proper service procedures must be followed without exception. High voltage is deadly and unforgiving.

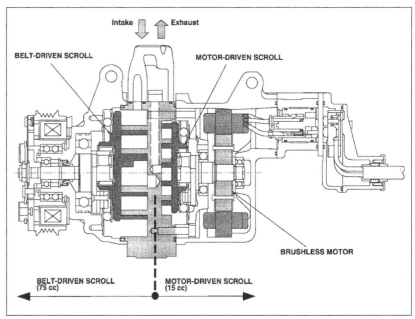

Electric Compressor Components

COMPRESSOR CLUTCH

The compressor clutch is an electromagnetic device which allows the compressor to be engaged and disengaged as necessary. Fixed displacement compressors will cycle the compressor off and on to maintain the correct temperature of the evaporator coil. Variable displacement compressor clutches are engaged at all times when the controls are set for A/C. The compressor clutch is monitored by various switches and controls to prevent system damage from a low refrigerant charge, a refrigerant overcharge, or low ambient temperatures. The compressor will also be disengaged during certain engine operating conditions such as wide open throttle or high power steering system pressure.

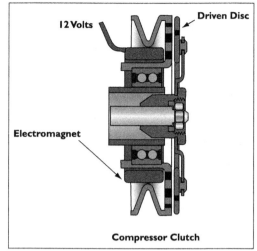

Compressor Clutch

Cycling Clutch Designs

Most clutches are made up of three primary pieces: the field coil, which is mounted to the face of the compressor; the pulley assembly, which is mounted on a bearing to the nose of the compressor; and the drive belt which turns the pulley. The clutch drive plate is attached to the compressor drive shaft. The drive plate is the movable piece that will be engaged or disengaged to turn the pistons, vanes or scroll in the compressor case. The clutch pieces will be held together with snap rings, screws or press fit to keep the unit together. An air gap must be maintained between the pulley and the drive plate. The air gap is adjusted with shims or through a press fit between the drive plate hub and the compressor driveshaft. Some clutches will be equipped with a thermal fuse. Most clutch field coil electrical circuits are equipped with a diode to protect the vehicle's electronics from voltage spikes.

Clutch Components

BREAK-AWAY HUB OR DAMPER DRIVE DESIGNS

Some variable displacement compressors are designed to run constantly. If the compressor seizes, the drive belt would break and additional vehicle systems such as the water pump and generator could be affected. To prevent damage to the drive belt and allow operation of the other vital components, the compressor drive plate is designed to break free or it may have a torque limiting hub that will disengage the drive plate from the pulley assembly.

Break-away Design

Condenser (shown in vehicle)

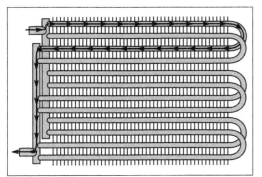

Refrigerant Flow through Condenser

Condensers

The condenser is a heat exchanger that is used to convert the pressurized refrigerant gas into a liquid. Similar in design to a radiator, the condenser consists of refrigerant tubing mounted in a series of thin cooling fins. Most condensers are mounted in front of the radiator where airflow is produced by the movement of the vehicle or by fans that are mounted behind the condenser to help draw air through the condenser during idle and low speed operation.

Refrigerant enters the condenser through the discharge line from the outlet side of the compressor. The refrigerant is a high-pressure hot gas, which can reach pressures as high as 420 psi (28.5 bar). The refrigerant vapor enters the top of the condenser and flows through the tubes toward the bottom of the condenser. Depending on the condenser design, the refrigerant will travel back and forth or in a parallel flow.

The air flowing through the condenser is lower than the temperature of the heat stored in the refrigerant vapor. Because heat always moves from a warmer area to a cooler area, the heat flows through the tubes and fins of the condenser to the outside air. As the heat is released, the refrigerant changes state from vapor to liquid. This process is known as condensation.

Under normal conditions, the condenser contains hot refrigerant vapor in the top two-thirds of the tubes and warm liquid refrigerant in the lower third. Condensation is a constant process as long as the A/C is operating. Although the condenser has no moving parts, it is a critical component of the A/C system. Condenser problems can occur due to leaks, internal restrictions, and restricted airflow. Condensers are made in a variety of designs depending on the vehicle manufacturer, model year and model.

Notes:

TUBE-AND-FIN CONDENSERS

For many years prior to the introduction of R-134a, the 3/8-inch diameter round tube-and-fin condenser was the performance standard. This design still covers a portion of the aftermarket for older vehicles. Since cars and trucks are remaining on the road longer, the 3/8-inch tube-and-fin is not going away completely. However, in the last days of R-12, vehicle manufacturers were looking to improve efficiency and reduce system refrigerant charge amounts. That led to increasing use of four newer, more efficient types of condensers: the serpentine, the 6-mm piccolo, the multi-flow and the multi-flow with subcooling.

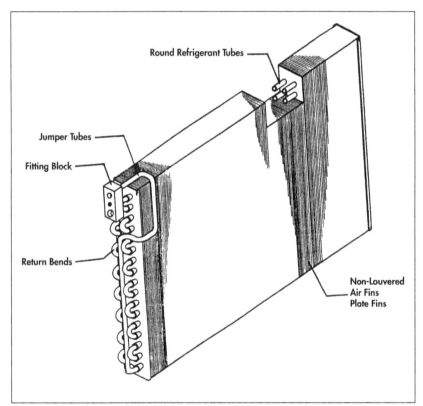

Tube-and-Fin Condenser Components

NOTES:

Serpentine Tube Condenser

The serpentine tube design has a snake-like shape to the tubing from inlet to outlet. Most serpentine condenser tubes contain several passages. A modern serpentine condenser is about 15 percent more efficient than a 3/8 inch-tube-and-fin.

Serpentine Tube Condenser

6-mm "Piccolo" Condenser

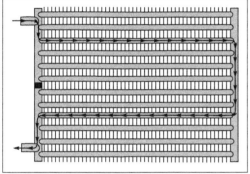
Flat Tube Multi-flow Condenser

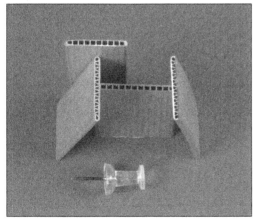
Refrigerant Tubes

6-mm "Piccolo" Condensers

There is approximately a 1/8-inch difference in diameter between the tubing in a 3/8" tube-and-fin design and a 6-mm "piccolo" design. As a result, the 6-mm piccolo design contains more refrigerant tubes in less space. Built with internal baffles in the manifold pipes, it is a version of multi-flow design. As a result of these design changes, it provides more efficient heat transfer than the larger conventional tube-and-fin design.

Flat Tube Multi-flow Condensers

Flat tube multi-flows are considered to be the most efficient design in use. The flat tubes provide more surface area to expose the refrigerant to the cooler air flowing through the air fins. They are continually being re-designed to make them even more efficient. The refrigerant tubes are getting smaller while the number of passages have increased. This allows the refrigerant flow to break into tiny streams, which will release heat rapidly. The passages in these designs are now so tiny that they can be plugged by small particles of debris.

If the tubes are clogged internally, attempting to flush them is not usually successful. The solvent will often bypass the blocked ports and flow through the clear passages, essentially taking the path of least resistance, and the blockage will remain.

Subcooling Condensers

Some vehicles will have the condenser and receiver/drier combined into a single unit. This design is called a subcooling condenser. A subcooling condenser has two sections, one is the condensing section and the other is the subcooling section. The receiver/drier is located between the two sections. The high-pressure, high-temperature refrigerant vapor is cooled in the condensing section to a mixture of vapor and liquid refrigerant. The liquid refrigerant is separated from the vapor in the receiver drier. Only liquid refrigerant enters the subcooling section. Subcooling the refrigerant ensures all the refrigerant will be in a liquid state before reaching the metering device ahead of the evaporator core.

Some condensers will incorporate additional coolers for the transmission or power steering. These components are part of the condenser and will be replaced with the condenser.

Subcooling Condenser (shown in vehicle)

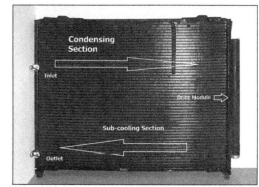

Subcooling Condenser Diagram

NOTES:

Evaporator

Evaporators

The evaporator is the other heat exchanger in a mobile A/C system. The evaporator is usually located inside the passenger compartment, inside the plenum which is the air distribution housing behind the instrument panel. The evaporator's function is to remove heat, dehumidify, and clean the air entering the passenger compartment. When the A/C system is operating, high-pressure liquid refrigerant flows through the expansion valve or orifice tube, after which the refrigerant's pressure and temperature drop. The low-pressure, low temperature, liquefied gas enters the evaporator core, and the evaporator becomes cold.

As the refrigerant changes from a liquid to a gas in the cold evaporator, it absorbs heat. Heat always travels from a warmer area to a cooler area. The blower motor pushes warm vehicle interior air through the evaporator fins. Because cooler air cannot hold as much moisture as warm air, condensed moisture forms water droplets on the evaporator surface. The droplets flow down the fins of the evaporator and exit through a drain tube at the bottom of the plenum. The moisture collects dirt, pollen, and dust that may be present in the airstream and washes it out with the water droplets.

Most modern evaporators are a plate-and-fin design. Spaces between the plates serve as the refrigerant flow passages. The plates are separated by air fins which absorb heat and condense the moisture from the air. The plates may be internally baffled to route the refrigerant back and forth across the width of the evaporator, providing more surface area to absorb heat. This design is more efficient than a tube-and-fin design that is used on some systems. Common problems related to evaporators include: plugged air fins, internal restrictions, leaks, excessive oil, and missing air seals.

Plate-and-Fin Evaporator

NOTES:

EVAPORATOR DESIGNS

The three major evaporator designs are the serpentine flat tube, plate-and-fin, and tube-and-fin. Evaporator improvements through the years have included changing the refrigerant flow path, changing the size of the refrigerant passages and modifying the air fin design to reduce air speed.

Evaporator refrigerant flow includes single pass and multiple pass. Single pass evaporators allow refrigerant to flow directly from the inlet to the outlet. Multiple pass evaporators direct the refrigerant flow back and forth across the evaporator several times from the inlet to the outlet.

Evaporator Designs

NOTES:

EMERGING EVAPORATOR DESIGNS AND NEW STANDARDS

Ejector Cycle System

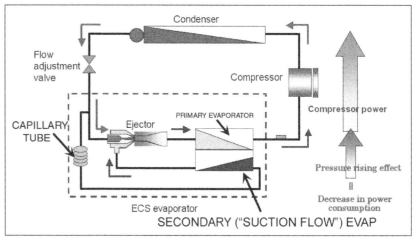

Ejector Cycle System

Starting with the 2010 model year, the Toyota Prius uses the ejector cycle A/C system and evaporator. The evaporator is designed like two separate evaporators face-butted together. It is referred to as a two-temperature evaporator, because each section cools air to a different temperature. The two air temperatures are mixed to provide the cooling requested through the control panel settings. The two-temperature evaporator combines the two evaporator sections, the ejector pipe and the capillary tube into a single, compact assembly.

The ejector is a device that without moving parts, recovers energy from operation of the compressor that is normally wasted when liquid refrigerant goes through the expansion valve and vaporizes. The shape of the ejector's piping results in a pumping action as the refrigerant flows through, and produces a pressure rise that represents recovery of the work that the compressor performed. At 77 degrees F., it recovers 11%; at 95 degrees F it recovers 18% and at 104 degrees F. it recovers 24%.

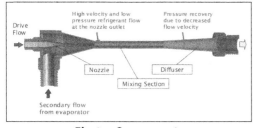

Ejector Components

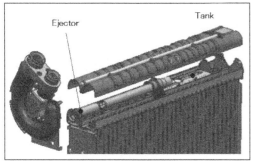

Ejector Location

As used in the Prius (and as it will be in vehicles to come), the system is familiar up to and including the expansion valve, except that in an ejector cycle system, the TXV is called a flow adjustment valve, so when liquid refrigerant flows through it, it drops a bit in pressure, but it doesn't vaporize. Just after the flow adjustment valve, the flow splits, with some of it going into a capillary tube (which limits the refrigerant flow rate) and then the flow continues through one of the two face-butted evaporator cores—cooling the surrounding air in the HVAC case. That's called the "suction flow," because it's actually drawn through the second evaporator by a vacuum produced in the ejector.

The liquid refrigerant enters the ejector through a tapered orifice within a pipe—that's the ejector. The shape of the ejector nozzle produces a rapid, jet-like refrigerant flow that creates a low-pressure zone (a vacuum, basically a venturi pump effect) in the immediate area surrounding it. That vacuum is what draws the refrigerant from the second evaporator up into the ejector pipe.

The suction effect from the secondary evaporator is half the picture. The other half – really the main one – is the flow of pressurized liquid refrigerant through the ejector pipe. After the refrigerant flow through the ejector nozzle creates the venturi effect to draw the refrigerant from the secondary evaporator, the dual flow – from ejector nozzle and secondary evaporator – continues into a straight pipe section. That's where the ejector nozzle refrigerant flow and the refrigerant from the secondary evaporator mix.

The mixed flow then continues to flow into a widened section of the ejector pipe. Because the section is wider, the refrigerant flow slows down and its pressure rises. At this higher pressure, it flows into the evaporator, where it vaporizes and absorbs heat. Because it's at higher pressure, however, its evaporation temperature is higher, so there's a bit less cooling from it, compared with what the "suction" evaporator produced. However, the two evaporators are face-butted, so the air temperatures mix and produce the required cooling.

The higher-pressure refrigerant flows to the compressor inlet, so the compressor has less work to do to bring it up to the required pressure.

THE J2842 EVAPORATOR DESIGN FOR R-1234yf REFRIGERANT

This standard was mandated by R-1234yf's mild-flammability. Evaporators must meet this "J" standard for structural integrity and corrosion protection. J2842 covers design certification for OEM and aftermarket-built evaporators. It requires that the evaporator have a label stating the unit meets the standard.

NOTES:

Refrigerant Lines and Hoses

Plumbing: Lines and Hoses

Refrigerant lines carry the refrigerant and trace amounts of oil between the refrigeration system components. Refrigerant lines are usually made of aluminum. Often the refrigerant lines will have rubber hoses crimped to them to provide flexibility and noise suppression. The hoses are made of different layers of material, each providing a specific function. Layers of rubber are used to provide flexibility. A layer of nylon helps prevent the refrigerant from leaking through pores in the rubber. A braided layer adds strength. A layer of butyl rubber covers the outside to protect the hose assembly from under hood heat, lubricants and fluids.

Refrigerant lines have distinct names and locations. The line that runs from the compressor discharge port is called the discharge line. It will always run from the compressor discharge port to the condenser inlet. The line that runs from the condenser outlet is called the liquid line. It is usually the smallest diameter line in the system. The third line is called the suction line. It runs from the evaporator or accumulator outlet to the suction port of the compressor.

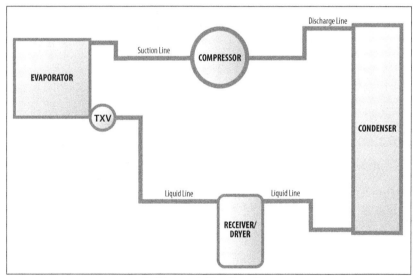
Refrigerant Line Routing

NOTES:

Mufflers and Filters

Mufflers are used on some A/C systems to reduce compressor pumping noises that result from the high-pressure or low-pressure vibrations at various operating conditions and engine RPM. Mufflers will often incorporate filters to protect the condenser from debris if the compressor fails. The most effective method of checking if a muffler is restricted is to perform a temperature drop test on the muffler. There should be no more than a 10° F difference between the muffler's inlet and outlet.

Mufflers

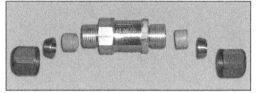

In-Line Filter

Connections and Fittings

- Captive
- Dual O-ring
- Spring-lock
- Flange or Block

Refrigerant lines and components use different types of connectors and fittings: O-ring, flange style, spring-lock, and sealing washers. O-ring fittings can be standard, captive, or dual. Always replace O-rings with those of the correct size. Lubricate the O-ring with mineral refrigerant oil and torque the fittings to the correct value.

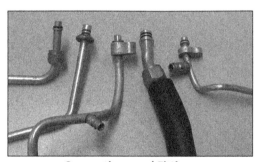

Connections and Fittings

O-ring Fittings

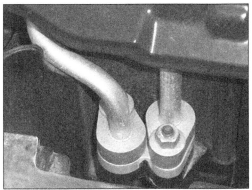

Flange Fittings Shown in Vehicle

Flange fittings, sometimes called peanut fittings, use either O-rings or gaskets between two metal flanges. If the gaskets have a rubber coating, the gaskets are installed dry. If the fitting uses O-rings, they should be lubricated with mineral oil. Flange type fittings must also be torqued to the correct value.

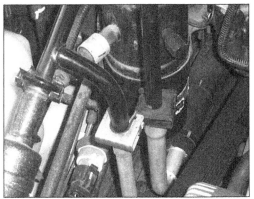

Spring-lock Couplings

Spring-lock couplings seal the connection using a sleeve that slides over a ferrule; two or three O-rings are placed in grooves on the ferrule to provide better sealing. The end of the sleeve is flared and slides into a cage at the end of the ferrule. The cage contains a garter spring that slips over the flare when it moves into the cage and hold it in place. A special service tool is used to disconnect this style fitting.

- Clean fittings
- Replace all O-rings/garter springs
- Lube with mineral oil or assembly fluid

Sealing washers improve leakage control; the sealing washers provide a more positive sealing surface than O-rings. Sealing washers are installed dry. Lubricating sealing washers will increase the possibility of contamination which may cause leaks.

- Install sealing washers dry
- Torque fitting to correct value

NOTES:

_____

_____

_____

_____

_____

_____

Service Ports

A/C systems are equipped with service ports that contain Schrader-type valve cores. These service ports will be located on the high-pressure and low-pressure sides of the system at various locations depending on system type and design.

R-12 equipped vehicles have externally threaded fittings; R-134a systems use quick-connect or "snap-couple" service fittings. The low-pressure side fitting is smaller than the high-pressure side fitting.

The service ports are equipped with a cap which serves as the primary seal for the service port. The service port caps must always be in place.

Service Port (shown in vehicle)

NOTES:

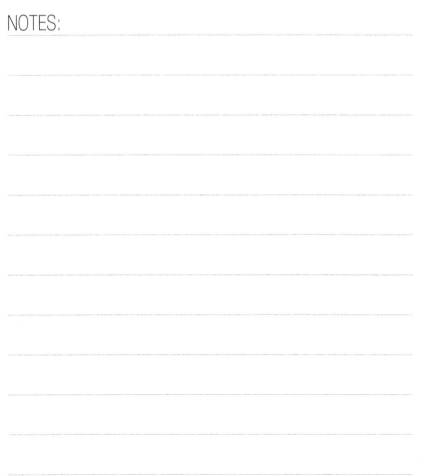

R-12 Service Port

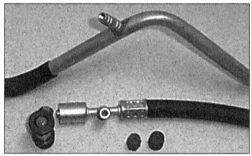

R-134a Service Port

SYSTEM DESIGNS: ORIFICE TUBE SYSTEMS

In an orifice tube system, the metering device that causes the pressure change of the liquid refrigerant is the orifice tube. The orifice tube can either be a fixed diameter or variable. The orifice tube is also incorporates a filter screen, and must be inspected and replaced during major repairs.

The accumulator is located between the outlet of the evaporator and before the compressor inlet. The accumulator is a liquid vapor separator and also contains a small filter.

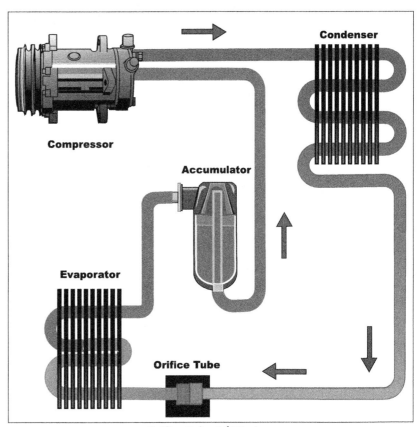

Orifice Tube A/C System

The orifice tube system can be a clutch cycling type when it is equipped with a fixed displacement compressor. The compressor clutch is cycled on and off according to the pressure or temperature on the low side of the refrigeration system. The compressor clutch can be controlled either directly by a pressure or temperature cycling switch or by the Powertrain Controller Module (PCM) using the pressure or temperature input. The PCM can also shut down the A/C compressor if it detects engine operating conditions that are out of range or will affect vehicle performance.

Typical Cycling Clutch Pressure Switch

The other system type is the constant-run design which uses a variable compressor. When A/C is requested, the compressor clutch will remain engaged until either the A/C system is turned off by the operator, or the PCM turns off the clutch.

Orifice Tubes

An orifice tube is a free flowing device that separates high- and low-pressure sides of the system. It is located in the liquid line between the outlet of the condenser and the inlet of the evaporator. The orifice tube provides a restriction to the high-pressure liquid refrigerant that flows from the condenser, reducing its pressure as it meters the refrigerant into the evaporator as a low-pressure liquid.

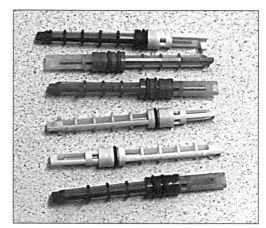

Orifice Tubes

FIXED ORIFICE TUBE DESIGN

The refrigerant flow rate through the orifice is determined by the diameter of the tube used. The tube size will usually range from .052" to .072" in diameter. The size of the orifice is matched to the evaporator volume and surface area. It is important that the correct replacement orifice tube is used to ensure proper system performance. The different sizes of the orifice are noted by the manufacturers by the color of the plastic housing. The orifice tube contains a filter screen on the inlet side of the tube to prevent contaminants from cycling through the system, and a diffuser screen on the outlet side. The refrigerant is further atomized as it passes through the diffuser screen.

If the orifice tube becomes restricted, the low refrigerant flow may starve the evaporator, causing insufficient cooling and possibly compressor failure.

Fixed Orifice Tube

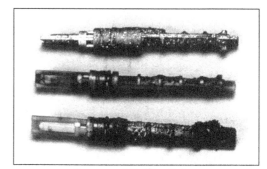

Damaged Orifice Tubes

NOTES:

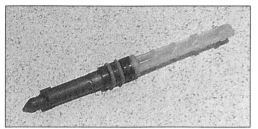

Variable Orifice Tube

VARIABLE ORIFICE TUBE

The variable orifice tube has two openings. One of the openings is fixed, the other will open and close based on the temperature of the refrigerant on the inlet side of the orifice tube. Under normal cooling loads, the refrigerant flows through the inlet filter screen, the fixed and variable ports, and both metering orifices. As the heat load on the A/C system increases, the temperature of the refrigerant entering the orifice tube increases, which causes the bi-metal coil to expand and restrict the flow of refrigerant through the variable port of the tube. Restricting the flow of refrigerant through the variable port provides a greater pressure differential between the high and low-pressure sides of the A/C system. This results in colder refrigerant vapor traveling through the evaporator. The colder refrigerant will absorb more heat.

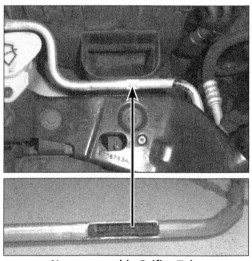

Non-removable Orifice Tube

NON-REMOVABLE ORIFICE TUBES

Some vehicle manufacturers, particularly Ford Motor Company, Chrysler Corporation, and Hyundai use a non-removable orifice tube that is crimped into the liquid line. To replace the orifice tube, the entire liquid line may be replaced or an orifice tube repair kit can sometimes be used.

NOTES:

Accumulator

The accumulator acts as a liquid-vapor separator that prevents liquid refrigerant from reaching the compressor. The accumulator also contains a desiccant for removing moisture from the refrigerant and a filter screen on the oil bleed hole on the suction tube that connects to the accumulator outlet.

As refrigerant enters the accumulator inlet, the liquid refrigerant falls to the bottom of the tank. Any moisture in the system will be absorbed by the desiccant. To prevent liquid refrigerant from reaching the compressor, the vapor return tube is positioned at the top of the accumulator tank. As the vapor rises it is pulled into the return tube by compressor suction.

Accumulators

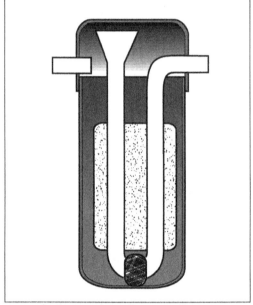

Accumulator Cross-section

The oil bleed hole is located on the bottom of the vapor return tube to draw in oil that falls to the bottom of the tank with the liquid refrigerant. The oil return is protected by the filter screen.

Accumulators should be replaced when:

• The system components are replaced.

• If the system has been left open for any extended length of time.

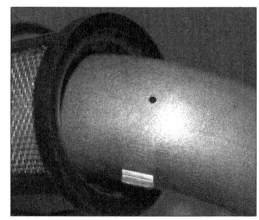

Oil Return Hole

THERMOSTATIC EXPANSION VALVE SYSTEMS

In an expansion valve system, the restriction in the metering device is variable. The expansion valve will regulate the amount of refrigerant entering the evaporator core, based on the temperature of the refrigerant exiting the evaporator. Regulating the amount of refrigerant in the evaporator prevents liquid refrigerant from reaching the compressor. The Thermostatic Expansion Valve (TXV) system uses a receiver drier located in the high-pressure side of the system to filter, store, and remove moisture from the liquid refrigerant.

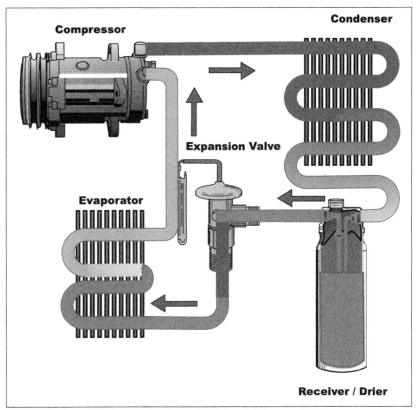

Thermostatic Expansion Valve System (TXV)

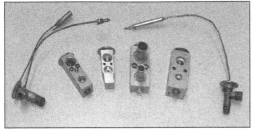

Thermostatic Expansion Valves

The expansion valve is located at the inlet of the evaporator core and separates the high-pressure side of the A/C system from the low-pressure side of the system. The amount of refrigerant that will enter the evaporator is based on the heat load which is determined by the expansion valve sensing element. Depending on the type expansion valve, it can be an external capillary tube and sensing bulb, or it may be a sensing sleeve which is placed internally in the refrigerant vapor flow that is exiting the evaporator.

To prevent the moisture collecting on the evaporator surface from freezing and blocking air flow, the evaporator core temperature must be kept above 32° Fahrenheit.

This is accomplished by using various switches and control valves. Thermostatic switches, pressure switches, and thermistors are used as inputs to control units (often PCMs, ECMs, BCMs, or dedicated A/C System control units) which, in most systems, cycle the compressor clutch on and off through a relay or Field Effect Transistor (FET).

Switches and Control Devices
used in TXV Systems

Variable displacement compressors are also used with TXV systems. Compressor output will vary to match heat load and prevent evaporator freeze up. These can be tricky systems to diagnose. The diagnostic test procedure must be followed to the letter to prevent replacing the wrong component.

Variable Displacement Compressor

NOTES:

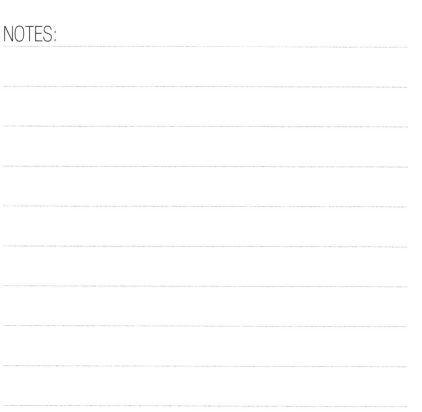

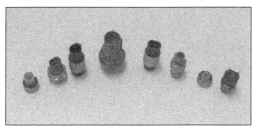

System Protection Switches

System Protection Switches

To protect the A/C system from very low or very high-pressures, as well as low ambient temperatures (compressor oil circulation may be affected in cold weather), various protection switches are used depending on compressor type and system design. There may be one switch with multiple tasks or several switches with specific tasks, such as a high-pressure compressor clutch cutoff switch or a high power steering pressure switch.

Thermostatic Expansion Valve

Thermostatic Expansion Valves

When the A/C system is operating, the TXV is performing three main tasks to ensure proper cooling and system operation:

- **Throttling** – the flow of the refrigerant is restricted or throttled by the valve. High-pressure liquid enters the valve, and low-pressure liquid leaves it.

- **Modulation** – the TXV adjusts the amount of low-pressure refrigerant liquid that enters the evaporator for proper system cooling.

- **Metering** – the TXV meters refrigerant volume according to changes in the heat load or temperature. Higher heat loads require more refrigerant to maintain optimum evaporator temperatures. Thermostatic expansion valves are made in various configurations to match the A/C system designs and vehicle requirements.

NOTES:

EL TXV Design

The EL ("L" shaped) valve shown here has an external sensing bulb that attaches to the outlet pipe of the evaporator. The sensing bulb must be correctly positioned and insulated in order for the valve to work properly. A capillary tube runs from the sensing bulb to a diaphragm chamber on the top of the TXV. The sensing circuit is a sealed subsystem that is charged with refrigerant. As the temperature at the outlet of the evaporator changes, the diaphragm will expand or contract against a push pin or pins inside the valve and these pins will move the seat assembly to increase or decrease the flow of refrigerant through the valve into the evaporator. Pressure from the refrigerant in the evaporator will be fed against the bottom of the diaphragm so the valve will operate smoothly. A superheat spring will push back against the seat assembly to also ensure smooth operation and to ensure that the correct amount of refrigerant will enter the evaporator to ensure proper heat absorption, and also to ensure that the refrigerant will be completely vaporized when it leaves the evaporator.

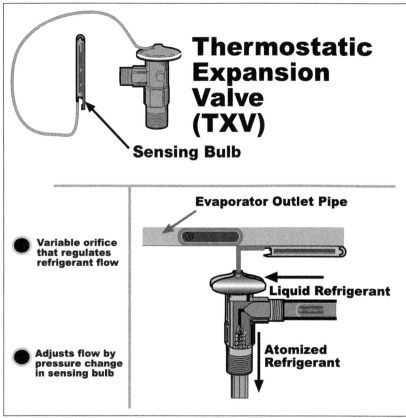

EL ("L" Shaped) TXV Design

NOTES:

H-Valve Design

The H-valve or block valve is another type of thermostatic expansion valve. This design consists of a four port body, control power dome (diaphragm), temperature sensing sleeve, push pin, ball and seat and superheat spring.

High-pressure refrigerant enters through the lower port and passes through the orifice where the pressure drops. After passing through the evaporator, the refrigerant exits the evaporator through the upper ports of the valve. The amount of refrigerant that enters the evaporator is based on the temperature of the refrigerant passing through the valve on the outlet side.

Refrigerant exiting the evaporator flows across the temperature sensing sleeve. The sensing sleeve is attached to the power diaphragm, which is sealed and charged with refrigerant. As the temperature of the refrigerant leaving the evaporator changes, the gas in the power dome will move the push pin and increase or decrease the flow of refrigerant through the orifice. The superheat spring pushes against the valve seat for smooth valve operation.

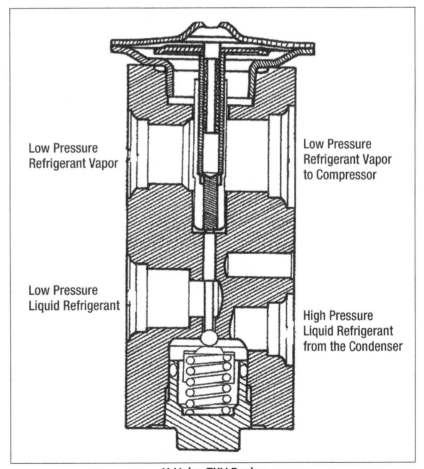

Low Pressure Refrigerant Vapor

Low Pressure Refrigerant Vapor to Compressor

Low Pressure Liquid Refrigerant

High Pressure Liquid Refrigerant from the Condenser

H-Valve TXV Design

Additional TXV Information

There are two different types of TXVs; externally equalized and internally equalized. Both EL and block (H) design valves can be of either type. A/C system pressure is applied to the bottom of the power dome or diaphragm so the push pins will operate smoothly. The externally equalized expansion valve has a separate evaporator pressure sensing tube connected to the evaporator outlet. Evaporator pressure travels through the tube to bear on the underside of the diaphragm. Internally equalized expansion valves contain an internal passageway that allows the back side of the diaphragm to be exposed to evaporator pressure.

Most TXVs have a slotted seat which prevents the valve from closing completely; this allows a small amount of refrigerant and oil to circulate through the system even if the diaphragm gas charge is lost.

TXVs should be inspected during major A/C system repairs. TXV's sensing bulbs can lose their gas charge, push pins can corrode and stick, the orifice can become clogged with debris and inlet screens (if equipped) can become clogged and restrict refrigerant flow.

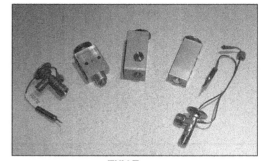

TXV Types

RECEIVER/DRIER

- Filters liquid refrigerant
- Stores liquid refrigerant
- Removes moisture from liquid refrigerant

A receiver/drier (R/D) is used on thermostatic expansion valve refrigerant systems. The receiver/drier is a cylinder typically installed on the high-pressure side of the A/C system between the condenser and the expansion valve inlet.

High-pressure refrigerant from the condenser enters through the inlet side of the R/D. The receiver/drier consists of a tank, filter, desiccant, and pick up tube. The R/D's purpose is to store, filter and remove moisture from the refrigerant.

As high-pressure refrigerant from the condenser enters the R/D, some of the refrigerant may still be in a gaseous state. This vapor will collect at the top of the R/D. Liquid refrigerant and oil pass through the desiccant and filter as they fall to the bottom of the tank. The liquid refrigerant and oil is drawn through the R/D outlet which is attached to a pick up tube positioned near the bottom of the tank so that only liquid is sent to the expansion valve.

Receiver/Drier (shown in vehicle)

Receiver/Driers

RECEIVER/DRIER DESIGNS

Conventional

Most receiver/driers are sealed canisters that are positioned between the condenser outlet and TXV inlet, in a location that will fit with the vehicle design and options. Sometimes the R/D will be inside the inner fender well or near the front cowl.

Receiver/driers have a distinct inlet and outlet. If the R/D is installed backwards, the A/C system will not function properly.

A sight glass may be located on the top of the receiver/drier or in the liquid line near the R/D. The sight glass is a visual indication of the refrigerant in the system. It should not be used in an attempt to determine the charge level in the A/C system.

Integral Receiver/Dryer (shown in vehicle)

Integral Receiver/driers

Integral receiver/driers are mounted on the condenser. Depending on the vehicle manufacturer, the drier may be non-serviceable and the condenser and drier is replaced as a single unit.

Other condenser-mounted desiccant packs can be replaced without replacing the condenser. Some also have a replaceable filter assembly.

Receiver/driers should be replaced whenever system has been opened for service. Most replacement compressor warranties require this.

NOTES:

REFRIGERANTS

Refrigerant is the life blood of an A/C system. Its continuous circulation as a liquid and a gas makes the system work. It transfers heat from one place to another. Heat is absorbed into the refrigerant in the evaporator and is released from the refrigerant in the condenser. Through the years, mobile A/C systems have used different refrigerants.

R-12

Most vehicles produced until 1994 used Refrigerant 12, called R-12, that was made of a chemical compound called a chlorofluorocarbon (CFC).

R-12 boils or vaporizes at -21.7° F. Maximum heat transfer takes place at the vaporization temperature. Because of this low boiling point R-12 made an ideal refrigerant.

However, studies found that when R-12 is released into the atmosphere, it breaks down in the upper atmosphere. The resulting free chlorine atoms damage the ozone layer. The ozone layer is located in the stratosphere and protects the planet from the harmful effects of the sun's ultraviolet radiation. Because of these findings, the automotive industry adopted a safer refrigerant.

R-12 Refrigerant Canister

R-134a

R-134a is a Hydrofluorocarbon (HFC) that does not contain chlorine. R-134a vaporizes at -15.0° F. R-134a is the refrigerant of choice for retrofit on R-12 systems.

Starting with a limited number of vehicles in 1992, and completed by 1995, all mobile A/C systems were changed to work with R-134a refrigerant which continues through current production. R-134a is classified as contributing to global warming, but does not deplete the ozone layer. As a regulated substance it must be recovered and recycled. Concerns regarding the global warming potential of HFC- 134a led the European Union to ban its use in mobile air conditioning starting in 2011. R-134a has a Global Warming Potential (GWP) of 1410.

R-134a Refrigerant Canister

European governments are requiring the use of a refrigerant with a GWP of less than 150. Several alternative refrigerants were reviewed and a consensus was reached on a substance known as R-1234yf.

R-1234yf

R-1234yf may also be called tetrafluoropropene. The GWP for R-1234yf is only 4 and its cooling characteristics are similar to R-134a's; the boiling point for R-1234yf is -20.2° F. Testing to date has found that the same desiccant type and quantity used with R-134a will work with R-1234yf. The current indications are that PAG oil will be used with R-1234yf, however current R-134a PAG oils will not work with R-1234yf. R-1234yf cannot be used to retrofit R-134a systems.

R-1234yf tanks will white with a red stripe at the top. The tank valve will be unique to prevent cross contamination.

The European roll out for R-1234yf is to begin in 2011. It must be used on any new vehicle type and will be phased in completely by 2017.

GM announced that it will use R-1234yf in some of its North American fleet beginning with the 2013 model year.

NOTES:

Refrigerant Identification and Testing

The quality of the refrigerant in the A/C system can affect performance. Other gasses, such as air or mixed refrigerants, will have different evaporation and condensation ranges and will change the amount of heat that can be removed.

SAE International recommends that usable refrigerant should not contain more than 2% concentration by weight of non-condensable gas (air). If the refrigerant in the system contains excessive air only, the excess air can be removed and the refrigerant can be used.

If the system has blends of refrigerants, the contaminated refrigerant must be removed with recovery equipment and disposed of in accordance with EPA regulations.

The only way to accurately determine the amount of air or contaminants contained in refrigerant is to use a refrigerant identifier or diagnostic tool.

Contamination caused by mixed refrigerants can produce readings mimicking air contamination.

A refrigerant identifier is the best tool to use to obtain a reading on the amount of air that might be in recycled refrigerant.

Refrigerant Diagnostic Tool

NOTES:

NOTES:

Recovery and Disposal of Contaminated Refrigerant

Under federal law, contaminated refrigerant cannot be vented. Recovery/recycling equipment is not designed to recycle or separate contaminated refrigerants. Contaminated or unknown refrigerant must be removed from a system using dedicated recovery-only equipment, and properly disposed of.

There are currently two types of equipment that can be used to recover contaminated refrigerant:

• Recovery-only units offered by some equipment manufacturers that are specifically designed for this purpose;

• An R-12 or R-134a recovery unit can be specifically dedicated for the purpose of recovering contaminated refrigerant.

Caution: If the refrigerant contains flammable substances, such as propane or butane, a fire or explosion could occur if the refrigerant is exposed to an ignition source within the equipment. Recovery equipment that has been certified for use with R-12 or R-134a is not approved for use with a flammable refrigerant and may become a safety hazard if used. Make sure you determine if features have been incorporated into your equipment to guard against these hazards.

Also, refrigerant containing flammable substances may be considered hazardous, and you must follow any local, state or federal requirements governing the storage and disposal of ignitable materials. (Visit *www.ecarcenter.org/ecartour.html* for more information on specific disposal requirements).

Contaminated refrigerant must be sent off-site to an EPA certified refrigerant reclaimer for either reclamation or destruction. A list of EPA certified refrigerant reclaimers can be found on the EPA's web site at *www.epa.gov/ozone/title6/608/reclamation/reclist.html.*

Or call the EPA hotline: 800-296-1996 for assistance.

Refrigerant System Lubrication

To ensure proper lubrication of the compressor, the correct amount and type of oil in the A/C system is important.

Too little oil will starve the compressor and increase its operating temperature. Too much oil reduces cooling performance, and can increase operating pressure and temperature, and may damage the compressor.

R-12 SYSTEM LUBRICANTS

Use mineral-based lubricants that are soluble with the R-12 refrigerant. Mineral oil is either 500 or 525 viscosity. Refrigerant oils are highly refined products and must be handled with care. The container cap must be kept clean and tight when not in use.

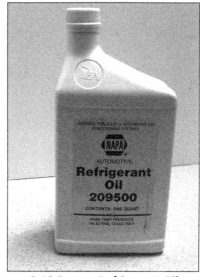

R-12 System Refrigerant Oil

R-134a SYSTEM LUBRICANTS

R-134a systems use several types of PAG lubricants. PAG oils are very hygroscopic, like brake fluid, and will absorb moisture from the air if left open. The container cap must be kept tightly closed to prevent moisture absorption. PAG oil can also damage painted surfaces; spills must be cleaned immediately.

To prevent damage to the compressor, it is important that the correct type and viscosity of lubricant (and correct amount) is used in an A/C system.

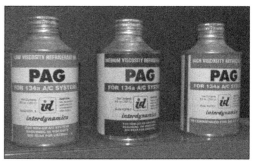

Polyalkylene Glycol (PAG) Lubricants for R-134a Systems

Do not mix lubricants. Use only the type of lubricant specified by the system manufacturer. The A/C system label will identify the vehicle, compressor or A/C system manufacturer's recommended lubricant, often by an OE part number or designation. If the label does not list the lubricant's viscosity, consult another information source such as a parts catalog or service manual to obtain the lubricant's viscosity rating.

Oil for Hybrids

HYBRID VEHICLE A/C SYSTEMS

Although hybrid vehicle systems use R-134a, electrically-driven compressors used on some hybrid vehicles require the use of special ester oil (POE) for lubrication. The electric compressor motor windings are immersed in the oil. If convention PAG oils are used, the oil may become conductive. Make sure to use the type of oil specified by the vehicle or compressor manufacturer.

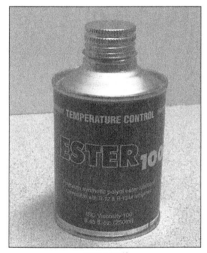

Ester Oil

LUBRICANTS AND RETROFITTING

The mineral oil used in R-12 systems does not mix with R-134a. Therefore, when retrofitting an R-12 system to use R-134a, to provide satisfactory compressor lubrication, it's necessary to add the proper viscosity and amount of synthetic oil to the system. In the vast majority of cases, the recommended oil will be a PAG lubricant. However, the compressors used on a few vehicles may require the use of polyol ester (POE) oil during a retrofit. The technician must consult appropriate service information to determine how much and which type of oil should be used. Each vehicle manufacturer has specific procedures in their retrofit bulletins. Note: The lubricants selected by the vehicle and compressor manufacturers were only tested and approved for use with R-134a as the retrofit refrigerant.

What about the Mineral Oil Already in the System?

Mineral oil and synthetic lubricants are compatible in a system. Since the mineral oil is not miscible with R-134a, it will typically harmlessly collect in different parts of the system.

Some vehicle manufacturers recommend removing as much of the original oil as possible by draining the compressor and replacing the accumulator or receiver/drier. However, the removal of mineral oil is not required by most vehicle manufacturers.

REFRIGERANT ADDITIVES

Most vehicle manufacturers do not recommend the use of additives or A/C system "enhancers." However, the aftermarket offers various products in these categories. Often, the use of these products will void warranties from the vehicle manufacturer or replacement parts suppliers. The SAE (Society of Automotive Engineers) International has issued a standard applicable to mobile A/C system additives and other chemicals intended for use in mobile A/C systems, SAE J2670.

SAE J2670: "Stability and Compatibility Criteria for Additives and Flushing Materials Intended for Use in Vehicle Air-Conditioning Systems Using R-134a"

The purpose of this standard is to provide testing and acceptance criteria to evaluate the stability and compatibility of chemicals, including flushing materials and additives (e.g., to enhance lubrication, durability, cooling performance, energy performance, prevent/fix leaks) intended for use in R-134a vehicle air conditioning systems. Successful completion of all requirements contained in this specification indicates acceptable compatibility with the A/C system materials, but does not suggest that the additive improves system performance in any way.

SAE Label

This SAE standard applies to any and all additives and chemical solutions intended for aftermarket use in the refrigerant circuit of vehicle air-conditioning systems. This standard provides testing and acceptance criteria for determining the stability and compatibility of additives and flushing materials (solutions) with A/C system materials and components, that may be intended for use in servicing or operation of vehicle air conditioning systems. This standard does not provide test criteria for additive, compressor lubricant, or flushing solution effectiveness; such testing is the responsibility of the additive and/or solution manufacturer/supplier. It is not the intent of this document to identify the requirements for Standard J2297 Ultraviolet Leak Detection: Stability and Compatibility Criteria of Fluorescent Refrigerant Leak Detection Dyes for Mobile R-134a Air-conditioning Systems. All leak detection materials must meet the requirements of J2297.

Section 3: Retrofit – Background and Overview

NOTES:

BACKGROUND

Concern about possible depletion of the ozone layer from CFCs was first raised in 1974. Research indicated that chlorine released from CFCs could migrate to the stratosphere and destroy ozone molecules. R-12 was the refrigerant of choice through the 1990s.

Before the 1990s, it was common practice to add refrigerant to leaking systems. It was also common practice to vent the entire refrigerant charge to the atmosphere if the refrigeration system required any type of service. These practices were acceptable because refrigerant was relatively inexpensive and thought to be environmentally benign.

To protect the ozone layer, the United States, and over 180 other nations ratified the 1987 Montreal Protocol on Substances which deplete the Ozone Layer. This landmark international agreement is designed to control the production and consumption of certain chlorofluorocarbon and halon compounds. With the advent of the Montreal Protocol, the Mobile Air Conditioning industry changed to R-134a. By late 1994, all new mobile air conditioning systems produced in the United States used R-134a.

Knowing what we do today about the role of R-12 in the degradation of the earth's protective ozone layer, and the potential of global warming, venting refrigerants is irresponsible and is not permitted. Under the Clean Air Act, this activity is illegal. In other rulings, the EPA prohibits the venting of other refrigerants, including R-134a and blend refrigerants used in mobile air conditioning systems.

R-12 has both an ozone depleting and global warming potential (GWP). R-134a is not ozone depleting but is considered to have global warming potential.

Blend refrigerants that were listed as acceptable by the EPA for servicing mobile air conditioning systems are also covered by the non-venting requirements.

OVERVIEW
Blends and Flammable Substances

When R-12 was initially phased out as the refrigerant of choice in new mobile A/C systems, it was thought that R-134a would not be compatible with the R-12 system designs and components. Many companies began to develop replacement refrigerants for the R-12 systems. Most replacement chemicals were blends of different refrigerants or, in some cases, flammable substances. Each chemical required different service fittings, service equipment and different retrofitting procedures. This created some problems for the service industry. For example, a repair facility would have to have several pieces of additional equipment for each product that was in the market place. (The use of flammable substances was banned almost immediately due to the danger of fire and explosion in the A/C system).

Unauthorized Refrigerant Blends

Damage from Improper Refrigerant Use

R-134a's Role

Fortunately, additional research and testing proved that R-134a could be used successfully in most R-12 systems. The key factors to retrofitting required the change to a synthetic oil, modifying the existing R-12 service fittings to R-134a service fittings, possibly replacing the receiver/drier to one with a different desiccant material, and the installation of a high-side pressure cutoff switch to prevent refrigerant from venting to the atmosphere. Installing a new service label indicating the amount of R-134a, the type of refrigerant oil used, and the name of the repair shop that performed the retrofit is also required.

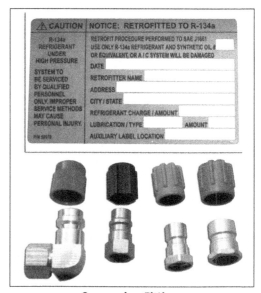
Conversion Fittings

R-1234yf

Given the chemical composition and cost of R-1234yf, and the required component design changes, this refrigerant will not be used for retrofitting R-134a systems. R-134a will continue in production until the R-134a equipped fleet is depleted. R-1234yf should never be considered for use in any system that was not designed to use it.

Section 4: Engine Cooling System Components and Operation

OVERVIEW

An engine cooling system consists of several components and has a direct affect on the operation and performance of the A/C system. During combustion, a tremendous amount of heat is produced. Approximately one-third of this heat produces the power to run the engine. Another one-third of the heat is lost through the exhaust system, and the remaining one-third is absorbed by the coolant passing throughout the engine components and passed through the radiator to prevent engine damage from overheating.

Some of the absorbed heat is passed through the heater core. This component is located in the HVAC plenum. The blower motor will force air through the heater core, directing the heated air through the ductwork inside the vehicle for passenger comfort, displacing cold air and safely defrosting the vehicle's windows. Besides removing excessive heat, the cooling system controls coolant flow to warm up the engine as quickly as possible and then maintains the correct operating temperature under all conditions. On most vehicles equipped with automatic transmissions, a transmission oil cooler is incorporated with the radiator to prevent the transmission fluid from overheating.

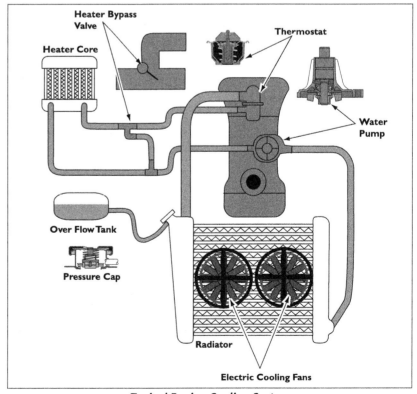

Typical Engine Cooling System

COOLING SYSTEM COMPONENTS

The operation of the engine's cooling system involves circulating a coolant through the engine passageways to absorb combustion heat, and pumping the hot coolant through the radiator to release that heat to the outside air. As an important support system of the A/C system, the cooling system has a number of components necessary for proper operation. Coolant can flow from the top to the bottom of the engine or from the bottom to the top, depending on manufacturer and engine type.

Coolant

Engine coolant is the liquid used to transfer heat away from the engine. It is a chemical that protects the engine from overheating, freezing, and corrosion. A properly maintained cooling system should contain a 50/50 mix of water and antifreeze. Use only distilled water or pre-mixed coolant. Do not exceed the 50/50 mix; although freeze protection will increase, there will be less protection to boil over in high ambient temperatures, as concentrated antifreeze is less efficient than water. Keep the cooling system full, and check the pressure cap for proper sealing and pressure range.

Keep an Eye on Coolant Level and Condition

CONVENTIONAL COOLANT

Engine coolant contains corrosion inhibitors that protect the engine and the cooling system components. There are different types of coolants used. "Conventional" coolant has been used for many years. It often contains silicates that form the protective barrier in the cooling system. Silicates in coolant can drop to less than original levels. This type of antifreeze must usually be replaced every two years or 24,000 miles.

Conventional Coolant

EXTENDED LIFE COOLANT

Organic Acid Technology (OAT) coolant, which contains no silicates, works in different way. Aluminum and ferrous metals will form a surface layer of corrosion when exposed to moisture. OAT coolants process this metal-oxide layer into a surface coating that protects against further corrosion. OAT coolants use organic acid rust/corrosion inhibitors, one called sebacate, another called 2-ethylhexanoic acid. The typical service life of OAT coolant is five years or 150,000 miles if the system coolant level is maintained correctly with a mixture of OAT coolant and distilled water.

Extended Life Coolant

OAT coolant is not compatible with some vehicle manufacturers' engine gaskets and other cooling system components. This led to the development of Hybrid Organic Acid Technology (HOAT) coolants. Most of these coolants contain low silicate content, no phosphates, and an organic acid inhibitor called benzoate. This coolant also has a five year, 150,000 mile life cycle when the cooling system is properly maintained.

COOLANT INSPECTION

Electrolysis is an electro-chemical reaction between dissimilar materials. This can occur when vehicle voltage is fed through the cooling system due to improperly grounded electrical components and decomposition of the vehicle's coolant. If electrolysis is suspected, the entire cooling system must be flushed and the entire vehicle electrical system tested to prevent it from reoccurring and causing premature component failure.

ELECTROLYSIS TESTING

Electrolysis Testing

The electrolysis test must be performed before and after cooling system service and repairs. Using a digital mulitmeter set on the 2 volt DC scale, attach the negative test lead to the negative battery post. Insert the positive lead into the radiator coolant. Do not touch the radiator core or radiator neck; the lead must be in coolant only. Any voltage reading over 0.3 volts indicates stray voltage is finding its way into the coolant. Electrolysis may be an intermittent condition, which can be caused by a poorly grounded electric cooling fan or other accessory. It can be checked by watching the volt meter, while turning on and off the various accessories or engaging the starter motor.

Notes:

COOLING SYSTEM FLUSHING

Cooling system flushing equipment can be either an all-in-one machine or a portable tool that works with standard flushing agents.

Both designs will leak check the cooling system and allow the system to be filled without creating any air pockets.

Using a flush machine is important. Your objective should be to remove at least 90 percent of the old coolant from a system. However, a long-quoted rule of thumb is that it can take up to three "drain and fill" operations with top up and coolant circulation to remove that amount (but the fact is it depends on how much old coolant comes out with each drain).

Draining only the radiator leaves 60-75 percent of the old coolant in the rest of the system. Removing the engine drain plugs greatly improves the percentage. However, there are many other components in the cooling system (for example, the heater core and the throttle body) that can still contain old coolant, and won't get emptied with a radiator or engine block drain.

Coolant with worn-out or depleted inhibitors promotes and accelerates system corrosion, particularly if the concentration is significantly lower than 50-50 because of dilution with plain water. If the coolant level is low, so the system contains air, problems can also include poor heater performance and air pockets forming around coolant temperature sensors, so they signal incorrectly. Filling modern cooling systems without possibly leaving air pockets is also not so simple. You can look for and open air bleeds, but they're sometimes not in plain view.

Back flushing may be required if the cooling system is restricted. It may contain more than rust or corrosion, perhaps also excessive sealer.

Bottom line: A good flush and fill machine is the most practical way to get out at least 90% of the old coolant, and refill the system quickly, efficiently and properly.

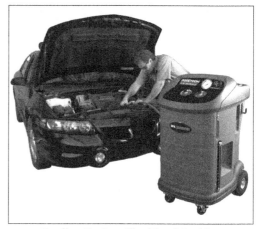

Cooling System Flushing Machine

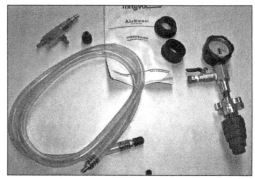

Cooling System Air Removal Device

Notes:

_____

_____

_____

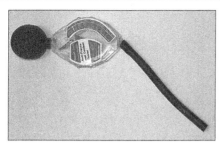

Hydrometer

Refractometer

Test Strips

TESTING COOLANT MIXTURES

Hydrometers can be used to check the concentration of conventional coolants.

Use a refractometer to check all other coolants since the specific gravity of propylene glycol has a density close to water. The refractometer will work with any antifreeze/coolant.

Test strips measure the concentration of the antifreeze coolant inhibitors in the cooling system. Test strips will measure mixture condition, freeze levels, reserve alkalinity, and pH levels. Test strips are available for all types of coolant.

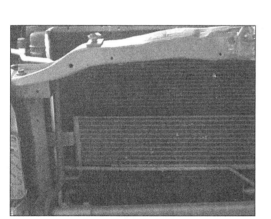

Crossflow Radiator

Downflow Radiator

Radiators

The radiator is the cooling system's heat exchanger, usually located behind or beside the A/C condenser. As ambient air passes through the radiator core, the engine heat is transferred from the coolant to the outside air. In most A/C system designs, the air conditioning condenser is mounted in front of the radiator. Turbocharged engines often have a charge air cooler, or "intercooler" mounted between the A/C condenser and the radiator. Other heat exchangers, such as transmission fluid and power steering coolers, may also be located with the radiator and A/C condenser. If the cooling system is not working properly, not only engine overheating, but poor A/C performance, transmission operation and engine performance could result.

Radiators used on modern vehicles are either crossflow or downflow design, and usually made of plastic and/or aluminum.

PRESSURE CAP

The pressure cap seals and pressurizes the cooling system, which allows operation at high temperature without loss of coolant. The cap maintains system pressure, which raises the boiling point of the coolant approximately 3° F per 1 psi of pressure. The pressure cap is also designed with a vacuum relief to prevent air from being drawn into the cooling system when the vehicle is stopped and the engine cools down. Always test the function of the pressure cap when testing the cooling system. Replace the cap if it cannot hold the specified pressure. Always clean the cap and sealing surfaces before replacing the cap to ensure proper sealing.

Pressure Cap - Top

Pressure Cap - Bottom

Coolant Recovery and Pressure Tank

Usually mounted near the radiator is a storage tank that allows for expansion of the coolant during operation and ensures that no air enters the cooling system. The recovery tank is connected to the radiator with a hose. Many late model systems have the pressure cap on the tank. This style is often called a surge tank. Both designs allow the coolant level to be checked at the tank. However, during system troubleshooting, if present, the cap on the radiator filler neck should be removed and coolant level checked in the radiator. The coolant recovery tank must be removed and cleaned when the cooling system is flushed.

Coolant Storage Tank

Notes:

Thermostat

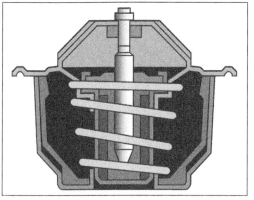

Thermostat Cross Section

Thermostat

The thermostat is a valve that controls the flow of coolant between the engine and the radiator. Located in a coolant passage near the top or bottom of the engine, the thermostat holds the coolant in the engine until a predetermined temperature is reached after a cold start to allow the engine to warm up quickly.

A wax pellet element in the thermostat expands when heated and contracts when cooled. The pellet element connects through a piston to a valve. When the pellet element is heated, pressure is exerted against a diaphragm which forces the valve open. As the element is cooled, the contraction allows a spring to close the valve. The opening and closing of the thermostat permits enough coolant to enter the radiator in order to keep the engine within operating range. Using the correct thermostat is essential for proper engine operation and emission standards. OBD II systems will monitor the thermostat for proper operation.

Notes:

Coolant Pumps

A centrifugal water pump circulates coolant through the water jackets, passages, intake manifold, radiator core, cooling system hoses and heater core. The pump is usually driven from the engine crankshaft by a belt, or by the engine timing belt or chain. The water pump impeller is pressed onto the rear of a shaft that rotates in bearings pressed into the housing. The housing has small holes to allow minor seepage to escape. The water pump seals are lubricated by the antifreeze in the coolant mixture. Overheating can occur if the drive belt is worn or the belt tensioner fails, causing the coolant pump to slow or stop. These drive systems must be properly maintained.

Coolant Pump

Air Intake System Components

Baffles and fan shrouds are designed to ensure maximum airflow through the A/C condenser and radiator for maximum cooling. Baffles are usually mounted on the sides of the condenser and between the condenser and radiator supports. Missing baffles will cause a portion of the air to bypass the condenser/ radiator and reduce cooling. Missing baffles must be replaced. Air dams, located under the bumper, are often damaged by road debris and parking curbs. Missing air dams allow ram air to flow under the vehicle instead of through the condenser/radiator, leading to overheating or poor A/C performance.

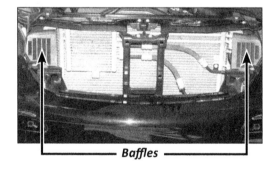

Baffles

Notes:

Cooling Fan

Cooling Fans

As the vehicle moves forward, ram air will pass through the condenser and radiator and remove heat. Often, there is not enough air flow to provide adequate cooling. Cooling fans are used to increase airflow during high ambient temperatures, stop and go driving, and high heat loads such as increased humidity and heavy traffic at slow vehicle speeds. Various cooling fan designs are used depending on vehicle model and year.

Viscous Cooling Fan Clutch

VISCOUS COOLING FANS

Viscous fans are driven by a belt. The viscous fan clutch is a three-piece device with a drive member attached to the water pump shaft, a driven member attached to the fan blades, and a control vane. The control vane usually has a bi-metal spring in front of the driven member. As the temperature of the airflow through the radiator increases, the bi-metal spring will react and allow silicone fluid to flow from a reservoir to passageways between the drive and driven members to increase fan speed to increase cooling. Viscous fans can rotate clockwise or counterclockwise depending on the routing of the drive belt over or under the water pump pulley.

Electronic Viscous Cooling Fan

ELECTRONIC VISCOUS COOLING FANS

Some vehicles use a viscous fan that is controlled through the engine or powertrain electronic controller. The control vane uses a pulse width modulated solenoid in place of a bi-metal spring to regulate the flow of silicone between the drive and driven members of the fan drive. The engine controller monitors engine coolant temperature, intake air temperature, A/C system pressure, transmission fluid temperature and possibly other parameters, and adjusts fan speed based on these values. If fan speed is out of range, or operating circuit wiring values are incorrect, Diagnostic Trouble Codes (DTCs) will set. A scan tool is used to read the DTCs and check fan solenoid operation.

Notes:

HYDRAULIC COOLING FANS

Hydraulic fans are located between the radiator and the engine. The power steering pump or dedicated pump supplies hydraulic fluid to a hydraulic motor to rotate the cooling fan blades. The amount of fluid that enters the hydraulic motor determines fan speed. The PCM controls the hydraulic cooling fan motor solenoid. The PCM will monitor ambient air temperature, A/C system pressure, engine coolant temperature, transmission fluid temperature and other inputs to determine fan speed. The solenoid is controlled by Pulse Width Modulation (PWM). The PCM will set DTCs if the fan controller is out of range.

Hydraulic Cooling Fan Motor

ELECTRIC FANS

Electric cooling fans can be controlled based on information from various sensors or inputs from the A/C system. Different vehicles use different strategies for cooling fan operation. On vehicles with a single speed fan, the fan may come on when the compressor clutch is engaged, or when coolant temperature reaches a predetermined value. On vehicles using one dual speed fan, the fan will operate on low speed when heat load reaches a predetermined point. As coolant temperature increases or A/C high side pressure increases, the fan will switch to high speed. If temperatures get too high, the compressor clutch will turn off and the cooling fan will continue to operate at high speed. Vehicles with two fans may operate one fan on engine coolant data and the other from A/C system pressure data. Both fans may operate together if the heat load is high enough.

Electric Fan

Fans may be controlled by relays or a fan controller that will operate the fans through pulse width modulation. Electronically controlled fans usually turn off when the vehicle reaches about 40 mph.

FAN COMBINATIONS

Some vehicles use a combination of engine driven and electric fans. Depending on strategies, the primary fan may be the engine driven fan, and the electric fan is secondary. Or the electric fan may be primary and the engine driven fan secondary.

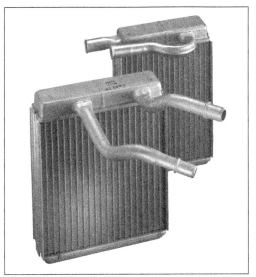

Heater Core

Heater Core

This heat exchanger is usually located under the instrument panel in a housing often called a "plenum." Hot coolant flows through the heater core to heat the vehicle's interior or to blend with air conditioned air to maintain a desired temperature in the various modes during all operating conditions. Excessive heat or lack of heat in any mode can be an indication of cooling system problems. Some heater cores fail due to corrosion and chemical erosion. Keeping the coolant changed and using distilled water helps to increase heater core life.

Heater Water Control Valve

HEATER WATER CONTROL VALVE

Some vehicles are equipped with a coolant shut off valve that can be operated mechanically, with vacuum, or electronically. The purpose of the valve is to prevent hot coolant from circulating through the heater core when maximum A/C cooling is selected. Heater valves can leak, become plugged, or stick open or closed, causing full heat or no heat from the HVAC module.

Flow Restrictor

FLOW RESTRICTOR

Some systems are equipped with a flow restrictor to prevent heater core erosion from coolant flowing through the heater core at a high speed. The restrictor also controls thumping noises in the heater core caused by the velocity of the coolant.

Coolant System Hoses

The cooling system components are connected through various hoses and lines. Radiator hoses are preformed and are attached to the engine and radiator by hose clamps. The heater core is connected to the engine and radiator by preformed rubber hoses or, on some vehicles, a combination of metal tubing and rubber hose. Hoses have a long service life if the cooling system is properly maintained. A major cause of hose failure is Electro-Chemical Degradation (ECD). ECD causes small cracks in the hose walls. ECD is generated by the different metals found in an engine which can cause small electrical discharges into the hoses. This can also be caused by an electrical system problem, such as a body ground strap missing or loose. The cooling system should be checked with a Digital Multimeter (DMM) for excessive voltage.

Coolant System Hoses (shown in vehicle)

Notes:

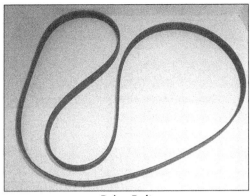

Drive Belt

Drive Belts and Timing Belts

Most modern vehicles use either a single drive belt or two drive belts to operate engine driven accessories. Multi-groove serpentine belts are most commonly used because they provide a large surface area, which helps prevent heat build-up and slippage.

Serpentine Drive Belt

Serpentine belts are usually tensioned through a spring loaded self tensioner. If the tensioner is weak or faulty, the belt can slip, causing improper operation of the alternator, power steering pump, water pump or any other belt-driven accessory.

Stretchy Drive Belt

Some vehicle manufacturers now use "stretchy belts" which eliminate the need for a self tensioner. The stretchy belt contains cords of compounds made with polyamide which gives the belt elastic qualities like a rubber band. Some of these belts are designed for one use only, and must be cut off to remove. A special tool may be required to install a new stretchy belt.

Notes:

Head Gaskets and Intake Manifold Gaskets

If a cooling system is not properly maintained, protective additives in the coolant may be depleted. The coolant may become corrosive and react with the materials used in engine gaskets, which will cause coolant leaks and affect engine performance and emissions.

Damaged Intake Manifold Gasket

If the cooling system is not pressurized at the correct value, the coolant level is not maintained, or the coolant has exhausted the additives, hot spots and corrosion can take place in the engine leading to head gasket, cylinder head, and core plug failures.

A weak cooling system will affect the other vehicle systems that depend on it for correct operation and durability. If an internal engine coolant leak is suspected, there may be white steam exiting the exhaust system, bubbles in the radiator coolant, or "mayonnaise" in the engine oil.

Head Gasket

Notes:

DIAGNOSIS AND TESTING

Cooling System Leaks

ULTRAVIOLET METHOD

Ultra Violet Test Equipment

A leak detection additive is available that can be added to the cooling system.

The additive is highly visible under Ultraviolet Light (UV). Pour the additive into the cooling system. Place the heater control unit in HEAT position. Start and operate the engine until the top radiator hose is warm to the touch. Aim the UV light at components to be checked. If leaks are present, UV light will cause the additive to glow a bright green color. The UV light can be used in conjunction with a system pressure tester to determine if any external leaks exist

PRESSURE TEST METHOD

Check the system cold if the cause of coolant loss is not located during the warm engine examination.

WARNING: Hot, pressurized coolant can cause injury by scalding. Never remove a pressure cap on a hot engine.

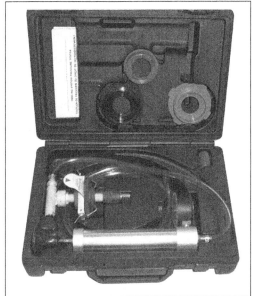

Pressure Test Equipment

Carefully remove the pressure cap from pressure bottle and check the coolant level. Wipe the inside of the filler neck and examine the lower inside sealing seat for nicks, cracks, paint, and dirt. Inspect the radiator-to-reserve/overflow tank hose for internal obstructions.

Inspect the cams on the outside of the filler neck. If the cams are damaged, seating of pressure cap valve and tester seal will be affected.

Attach a pressure tester to the filler neck. Operate the tester pump to apply the same maximum pressure to the system as the rating on the pressure cap. If any hoses enlarge excessively or bulge while testing, replace the hoses. Observe the gauge pointer and determine the condition of the cooling system based on the following criteria:

Pressure holds steady: If pointer remains steady for two minutes, no serious coolant leaks are present. However, there could be an internal leak that does not appear with normal system test pressure. If it is determined that coolant is being lost and leaks cannot be detected, inspect for interior leakage or perform internal leakage test.

Pressure drops slowly: This indicates a small leak or that seepage is occurring. Examine all connections for seepage or slight leakage. Inspect the radiator, hoses, gasket edges and the heater.

Pressure drops quickly: This indicates that serious leakage is occurring. Examine the system for external leakage. If leaks are not visible, inspect for internal engine coolant leakage.

Internal Leak Inspection

Remove the engine oil drain plug and drain a small amount of engine oil. If coolant is present in the oil, it will drain first because it is heavier than oil. An alternative method is to operate the engine for a short period of time. Afterwards, remove the dipstick and inspect it for water droplets Also inspect the transmission dipstick for water droplets.

WARNING: With the radiator pressure tester tool installed, do not allow-pressure to exceed 18 psi. Pressure will build up quickly if a combustion leak is present. To release pressure, rock the tester cap from side to side. When removing tester, do not turn tester more than 1/2 turn if system is under pressure.

Operate the engine without the pressure cap until the thermostat opens. Attach the pressure tester to filler neck. If pressure builds up quickly, this indicates a combustion leak exists. This is usually the result of a cylinder head gasket leak. If there is not an immediate pressure increase, pump the pressure tester. Do this until indicated pressure is 15 psi. Fluctuation of the gauge pointer indicates compression or combustion leakage into the cooling system.

Notes:

UNIQUE AND EMERGING COOLING SYSTEMS

To help reduce weight, improve fuel economy, and reduce emissions, various changes to the cooling system are being implemented.

Electric Coolant Pumps

Electric pumps, which have previously been used on auxiliary heating systems are being introduced on certain vehicles. Electric pumps improve coolant flow during certain operating conditions, provide engine off heating in hybrid vehicles, and help reduce emissions through improved cylinder temperature control.

Electric Coolant Pump

Multiple Thermostats

Some engines are using two thermostats to improve cooling efficiency and cold engine driveability. The additional thermostat may be located in the block, cylinder head or throttle body.

Multiple Thermostat Engine

Notes:

_____

_____

_____

_____

_____

_____

_____

Reverse Flow Cooling

In a reverse flow cooling system, the thermostat is located on the inlet side of the water pump. The coolant flows from the water pump to the cylinder heads, through the engine block. From the engine block, the coolant returns to the water pump and passes to the radiator. Reverse flow cooling systems usually operate at lower pressures.

Fail-Safe Engine Operation

Some vehicles are equipped with a fail-safe cooling strategy which allows the engine to operate without or with low coolant for a given range, usually 50 to 100 miles. The PCM will shut off the fuel injectors to alternating cylinders, and only air will be drawn in to the cylinders to keep the engine temperature down.

Fail Safe Cooling System Warning Light

Hybrid Cooling Systems

Hybrid vehicles have a separate cooling system for the electronics and batteries. The system can include an electric water pump to circulate coolant when the engine is shut off or when sensors detect high temperature conditions that require additional cooling of the power components of the vehicle.

The hybrid cooling system is not incorporated with the engine cooling system and is serviced as a stand-alone system from the engine cooling system.

Hybrid Cooling System

Air Delivery System

Section 5: Air Delivery Systems

INTRODUCTION

The air delivery system controls the movement of heated and cooled air into and throughout the passenger compartment. The HVAC housing is the plenum unit located behind and under the instrument panel. It contains the evaporator and heater core to provide clean, dry, cooled or heated air to the passenger compartment. The blower motor assembly and the blower speed control device vary the speed and volume of the airflow into the vehicle. The plenum connects to the air delivery ductwork that provides a pathway for the airflow to the correct areas in the vehicle. It also houses the air doors and door actuators that direct the air flow to the correct outlets of the ductwork. The doors can be controlled by cables, vacuum, or electrical actuators.

Blower Motor

The blower motor pulls or pushes air from the outside or inside the vehicle, through the heater core and the evaporator and into the passenger compartment through the various ducts and outlets. Located in the plenum, the blower motor is controlled through the control head (A/C and heater control panel).

Blower motor resistor types

Blower motor speeds are controlled with a resistor assembly or a control module. Resistor assemblies are wire wound, ceramic heat sink, or a credit card type.

The resistors are usually mounted in the plenum assembly downstream from the blower motor to keep the resistor assembly cool. Some resistor types have a thermal limiter that will melt if the blower motor circuit overheats. This will either shut down the entire blower motor circuit or allow high speed operation only.

Systems that use an electronic power module to control blower motor speeds will often use pulse width modulation to control blower speeds. The power module will usually be mounted in the plenum assembly like the fixed resistor assemblies.

Blower Motor

Wire Wound Resistor

Ceramic Design Resistor

Resistor Mounted on Circuit Board

• **Recirculation Door**. The recirculation door determines whether outside air is used in the plenum or recirculated air from the passenger compartment. The recirculation door will be located in the plenum air inlet. Most newer systems will not allow recirculation when the system is in defrost mode.

Recirculation Door

• **Blend Door**. The blend door position determines the temperature of the air flowing through the passenger compartment. If the A/C is operating, the air is dehumidified and cooled. The more air the blend door directs through the heater core, the warmer the air that enters the passenger compartment.

Blend Door

• **Mode Doors**. The mode doors determine where the air will be distributed. Most systems use at least two mode doors. One door opens and closes the defrost outlet. The other door switches between the heat and vent/normal outlets.

Mode Doors

• **Dual zone systems** operate in the same manner as single zone systems. However, most dual zone systems use two blend doors; one for the driver side and the other for the passenger side. This design allows for separate temperature settings on each side of the vehicle.

Dual Zone System

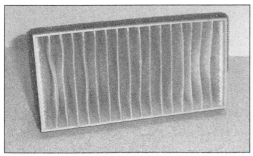

Cabin Air Filtration

- **Cabin air filtration** is now found on many vehicles. A filter will be located at the outside air inlet under the hood near the front cowl on some models. Other models will have the filter in the passenger compartment behind a removable door on the bottom of the plenum or behind the glove box. The filter removes dirt and pollen from incoming air and helps to control odors. If the filter becomes plugged, reduced airflow will result.

  Cabin air filters should always be changed in accordance with the vehicle manufacturer's scheduled maintenance recommendations.

Operator Interfaces

Operator Interface

All HVAC systems have a main component for controlling temperature, air distribution, and air speed from the vents. This component is the control head. It houses the various control switches, knobs, and levers that interface with the HVAC system. The control head will have a wiring harness for backlighting and for various inputs and outputs between the operator and the HVAC system. Electrical, mechanical cables, vacuum lines or a combination of these three are attached to the control head to control the various actuators on the plenum. The control head will provide some of the following inputs and controls. The number and types of switches will vary between make and model.

- A/C on-off switch: requests compressor clutch engagement.
- Temperature selector: adjusts outlet air temperature.
- Blower motor switch: multi-position switch that controls blower motor speed and air volume.
- Mode selector: routes airflow to different outlets and through various ducts.
- Recirculation switch: closes the outside air inlet for maximum system output.

NOTES:

Mode Controls

Where airflow will be delivered throughout the passenger compartment is selected on the control head. Mode selections may include: Maximum or Recirc, Normal or Vent, Bi-Level or De-mist, Floor or Heat, and Defrost. Controls may also be included for Rear A/C if equipped, and left and right occupant temperature control on dual control systems.

Mode Controls

Most new vehicles' control heads send an electrical signal to an electrical actuator which moves the flapper door to the selected position.

When the mode selector is moved from the off position, the blower motor and A/C clutch circuits are usually set to activate.

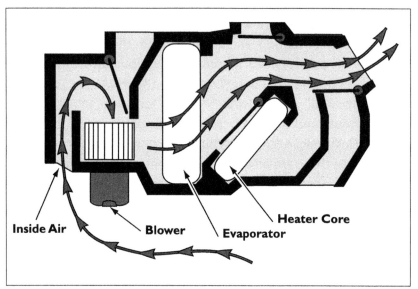

Max or Recirc Operation

Setting the selector to Max or Recirc allows for quicker cool down because outside air and humidity are restricted from entering the passenger compartment. It also helps keep unwanted outside odors from entering the cabin. Interior air returns to the blower motor air intake, is cooled and sent back into the passenger compartment.

NOTES:

NOTES:

In the Normal mode, outside air is drawn into the system.

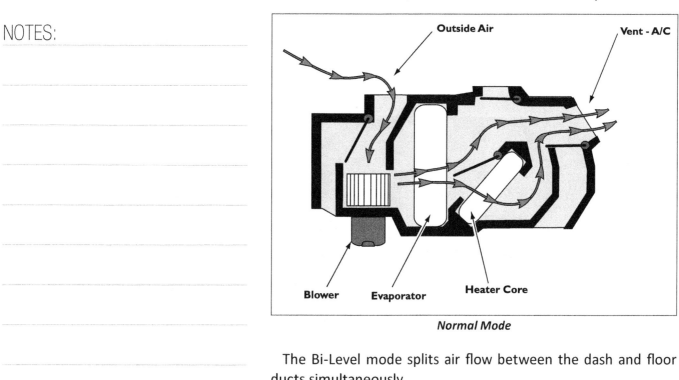

Normal Mode

The Bi-Level mode splits air flow between the dash and floor ducts simultaneously.

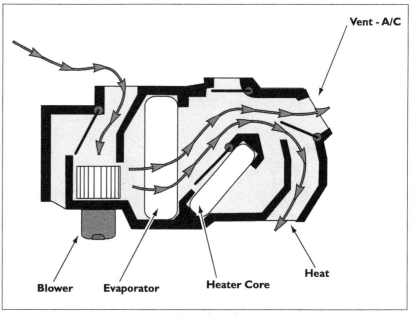

Bi-Level Mode

The Floor or Heat mode routes air through the floor ducts, usually with a small air bleed to the defrost outlets.

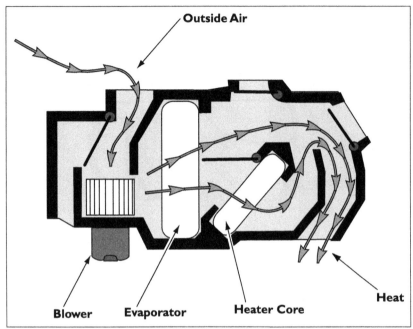

Floor or Heat Mode

The Defrost mode routes most of the air to the windshield outlets. In most vehicles equipped with air conditioning, the compressor is automatically activated when Defrost is selected. This allows for the most efficient windshield clearing.

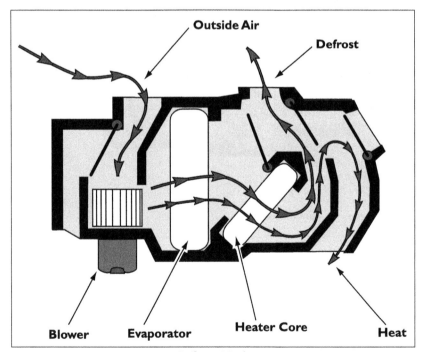

Defrost Mode

NOTES:

The temperature door directs the airflow through the evaporator and heater core and adjusts air temperature before it passes into the distribution ductwork. When the temperature door is in the closed position, all of the air is directed through the evaporator core. When the temperature door is open, air passing through the evaporator is also then directed through the heater core.

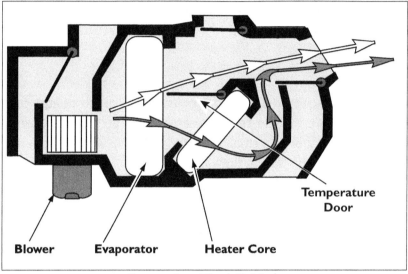

Temperature Door

Blower   **Evaporator**   **Heater Core**

Temperature Blend Air Mode

Vacuum Operated Heater Control Valve

Some vehicles use a heater control or bypass valve to control the flow of coolant through the heater core. The valve is usually located in the engine compartment, in the heater core inlet hose.

When the temperature control selector is in the full cold position, the heater control valve blocks coolant from flowing through the heater core. As the selector is moved to the warmer position, the heater control valve opens, and coolant flows through the heater core. The heater control valve can be cable, vacuum or electronically operated.

NOTES:

When a cable-operated heater control valve is used, as the temperature selector is moved, the heater control valve is manually opened or closed, adjusting the desired temperature.

On vacuum-operated systems, when the temperature selector is moved, vacuum is sent to the heater control valve, fully opening or closing the valve.

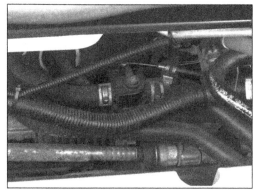

Cable-operated Heater Control Valve

Some newer systems use electronically-controlled heater control valves. Moving the temperature control on the dash sends an electrical signal to a small actuator at the valve. The actuator moves, opening or closing the valve.

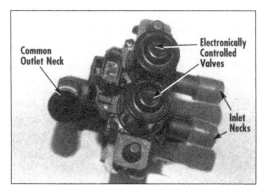

Electronically-Controlled
Dual Heater Control Valve

Mode Door Controls

Inside the case and duct assembly are doors or flaps, which change position to allow or block airflow to the desired outlets.

Mode doors can be controlled by cables, vacuum motors, or electric motors.

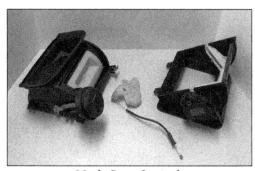

Mode Door Controls

NOTES:

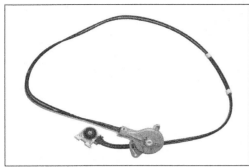

Cable Control

Cable controlled doors use a cable connected between the control panel and the mode doors. When the control is moved the cable transfers the motion to the mode door, either opening or closing it, and allowing air to flow to the corresponding vents.

Vacuum Actuator

Vacuum controlled doors use two designs; one utilizes a vacuum switch in the control head that directs manifold vacuum from a reservoir tank to the vacuum actuator attached to the door.

The other design uses vacuum solenoids; the electrical solenoids are grounded through the control head. When the desired mode button is pushed on the control head, the coil wiring in the vacuum solenoid box is grounded. When the coil is energized, vacuum flows from the reservoir tank to the vacuum actuator.

Electric Motor Actuator

Electric actuator controlled doors use a permanent magnet motor and gear set to move the door linkage. When the operator makes a change at the control head, current flows in the desired direction to move the door actuator motor. When current flows through the motor in one direction, the motor turns in a clockwise direction. When current flows in the opposite direction, the motor turns in a counterclockwise direction. The control head usually receives a signal that corresponds to door position. The controller will make adjustments to the door position to match the commanded setting based on the feedback value.

NOTES:

NOTES:

Section 6: Diagnostic and Service Equipment

INTRODUCTION

With any vehicle system service and repair, the necessary service equipment and tools are needed to make the correct diagnosis and perform the service or repair right the first time. A/C refrigerant systems are tested by reading the pressure on the high and low side of the system using gauges, performing temperature tests on the various system components, and measuring the temperature output at the center duct of the dashboard with a thermometer. These readings are compared to performance charts and standards established by the vehicle manufacturer.

If the A/C system is not operating correctly, additional tools such as a refrigerant identifier can check the condition and type of refrigerant in the system. A leak detector can check for refrigerant leaks. A refrigerant recovery, recycling, and recharging machine is used to remove, process, and recharge the system to the proper level. Additional tools and equipment are available through various suppliers. Read the operations manuals and follow the manufacturer's instructions when using any equipment.

A/C SERVICE, THE ENVIRONMENT, AND THE LAW

In the late 1980s R-12 refrigerant was identified as a major contributor to the depletion of the ozone layer that surrounds the earth. The chlorine contained in the R-12 reacts chemically with one of the oxygen atoms in the ozone molecule. New compounds of chlorine monoxide and free oxygen are formed. Neither can filter out the sun's ultraviolet rays. The increase in ultraviolet radiation results in increased health problems and disruption of the food chain. Studies have shown that 30% of the CFCs released into the atmosphere were coming from vehicle A/C systems. Some of the release was from leaks, but the majority of the release was during A/C service and repair. Since A/C service technicians have direct control over large amounts of refrigerants that could be released into the air, new service standards required recovery and recycling of all refrigerants used in mobile A/C systems.

In 1987, the Montreal Protocol was ratified, leading to the phase out of CFC based chemicals. In 1990, the Clean Air Act Section 609 gave the EPA authority to establish standards and requirements regarding servicing of mobile A/C systems. On July 14, 1992, it became illegal to vent chemicals used in mobile A/C systems into the atmosphere. On-site recovery of the refrigerant prior to service is required.

Since January 1, 1992 for R-12, and November 15, 1995 for R-134a and other mobile A/C refrigerants, any person servicing the mobile A/C pressurized circuit must comply with the Clean Air Act and must use either refrigerant recovery/recycling or recovery only equipment approved by the EPA. Any person who is receiving monetary value, which can include cash, credit, goods, and services, and who opens the refrigerant circuit must be certified by an EPA-approved organization to legally use such equipment to service the system.

Individual certification can be obtained through MACS Worldwide at 215-631-7020 or *www.macsw.org*.

NOTES:

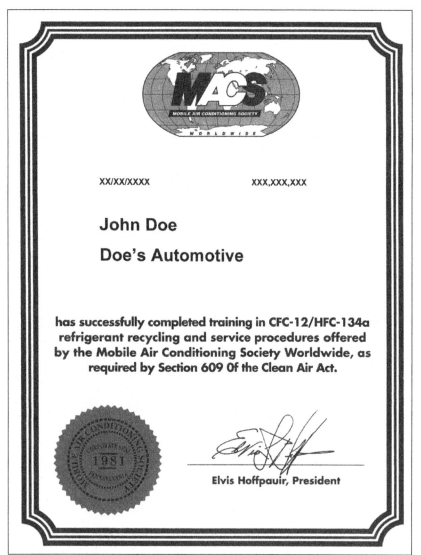

MACS Training Certificate

REFRIGERANT IDENTIFICATION AND TESTING

Sealant Detection

Sealant Detector

Several manufacturers produce A/C system sealants that are designed to stop refrigerant system leaks. There are primarily two types; one is designed to swell the O-rings and seals in the A/C system, while the other is an epoxy type of sealant that hardens when exposed to air or moisture. These sealants can cause component damage when used incorrectly. They can also clog refrigerant recovery machines and will void the machine warranty. Vehicle and component suppliers will void any warranties if this product is used. Tool kits that detect A/C system sealants are an important item to have and should be the first step when servicing an A/C system.

Recycle Guard. This device can be installed between the vehicle and the service hoses on the R/R/R machine to remove sealant, dye and oils.

Recycle Guard

Refrigerant Analyzers

Refrigerant Analyzer

The quality of the refrigerant in the A/C system can affect performance. Excessive air or a mix of refrigerants will reduce the amount of heat that can be transferred. The SAE has established standards for the purity of the refrigerant that can be used to service A/C systems. Several types of analyzers are available. The analyzer must meet the SAE J1771 standard to ensure proper identification and accuracy. The analyzers can check refrigerant storage tanks as well as in the A/C system. The refrigerant must be at least 98% pure and contain no more than 2% non-condensable gas (air). If the refrigerant is pure, but the percentage of air exceeds 2%, the refrigerant can be recycled to remove the excessive air.

If the refrigerant is contaminated with a mixture of different refrigerants or mixed with hydrocarbons, it must be recovered and disposed of properly. Contact the EPA at 800-296-1996 or on the web at: *www.epa.gov/ozone* for disposal locations.

Refrigerant Leak Detection

Electronic leak detectors are portable devices that can pinpoint refrigerant leaks as small as 0.5 ounce per year at a distance of 1/4 inch from the leak point for older units that met the SAE J1627 standard. New design electronic leak detectors that meet standard SAE J2791 can detect a leak of 0.15 ounce per year at a distance of 3/8 inch from the leak point. Electronic leak detectors must work with a minimum of 50 psi in the system. Follow the manufacturer's instructions for proper use.

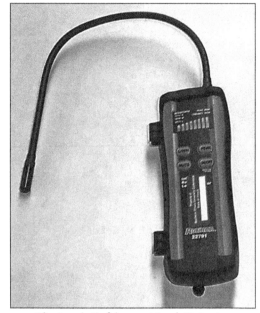

Electronic Refrigerant Leak Detector

Trace dye is a colored liquid added to the refrigerant system that mixes with the refrigerant oil and circulates throughout the system to locate leaks. After the dye circulates through the system for a period of time, the components, lines and fittings are inspected using a UV light which causes the dye to glow. There are various tools and methods for injecting the dye into the A/C system. Never add more than the recommended amount of dye to the system; excessive dye will cause system damage. Many vehicles come with dye installed during assembly. Check the service information to confirm if dye has already been installed.

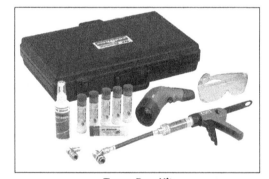

Trace Dye Kit

Manifold Gauge Set

A manifold gauge set is used to measure the high and low side pressures in the A/C system. The pressure readings are compared to the performance charts in the service information. The manifold set has two gauges, a manifold, hand valves, and service hoses. The low-pressure gauge will read both pressure and vacuum and is often called the compound gauge. The high side gauge will read pressure only. The gauge shells and service hoses are usually color coded, with blue for the low-pressure side and red for the high-pressure side. The center service hose is usually yellow. The ends of the service hoses will be equipped with shut off valves

Manifold Gauge Set

or quick disconnect fittings to prevent refrigerant escaping from the hoses when they are disconnected from the A/C system. During normal operation, the hand valves are in the closed position. Although gauges are now built into the refrigerant recovery, recycling, and recharging equipment, it is advisable to have an additional gauge set on hand to use with a stand-alone vacuum pump and refrigerant scale.

Thermometer

During the A/C performance test, a thermometer is used to measure the outlet temperature of the system. The thermometer probe is placed in the appropriate dash panel duct when the output temperature has stabilized; the temperature is compared to the value on the performance chart in the service information. Duct temperature will vary based on ambient temperature and heat load. The thermometer should be checked for accuracy by placing the temperature probe in a glass filled with ice and water. The thermometer should read close to 32° F if it is properly calibrated. This test should be performed on any thermometer, mechanical or electronic.

Thermometers

NOTES:

Temperature Testing Devices

Temperature testing should be one step in the diagnostic process and utilized with a performance test to help find A/C system problems or to confirm that the system is operating at peak efficiency after repairs. Temperature testing has been part of A/C system diagnosis since the beginning of A/C service and repair; the process involved touching the lines and components to check for a temperature change as the system was operating.

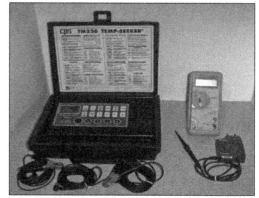

Temperature Testing Tools

In recent years, component suppliers and tool companies have developed specific test points and temperature values to indicate the condition of the A/C system. This research has led to improved A/C system performance and reduced component warranty claims due to poor lubrication and heat exchange.

Temperature testing is also an effective way of confirming that the A/C system is properly charged, by measuring the temperature difference between the inlet and outlet of the heat exchangers. Temperature testing also helps find hidden restrictions in lines and fittings.

Temperature testing can be accomplished using one of several tools. There are dedicated units from various suppliers. Plug in devices that work with a DMM are also available. Some DMM manufacturers will include a temperature probe with the lead kit.

NOTES:

Vacuum Pump

Vacuum Pumps/Micron Gauges

Two enemies of an A/C system are air and moisture. A vacuum pump is used to remove air by pulling the A/C system into a negative pressure. A vacuum pump may also be effective at removing some moisture from a system. When the system is brought into a vacuum, the boiling temperature of water is reduced. In order for the vacuum pump to work efficiently, its oil must be changed frequently. Some vacuum pumps will be equipped with a monitoring system that signals when it is time to change the oil.

Micron Gauge

MICRON GAUGE

The compound gauge may not provide an accurate reading during the evacuation process. The use of a micron gauge is recommended to ensure that a deep vacuum has been achieved. A reading below 500 microns indicates a deep vacuum.

NOTES:

Refrigerant Measurement Devices

Modern A/C systems must be charged with precision and accuracy. Electronic scales are available in two formats:

The strain gauge design measures actual weight. A refrigerant cylinder is placed on the scale, and the weight is monitored until the readout indicates the amount charged into the vehicle.

In programmable design, the refrigerant charge is dialed in and the scale turned on. The refrigerant charge is drawn into the vehicle, and the scale counts down the charge to zero. Both of these scales are used with a manifold gauge set. The hoses on the gauge set can hold 0.03 ounces of refrigerant per inch of length. This means that a typical six foot hose can hold approximately two ounces of refrigerant. The amount left in the hoses must be added to the system. This is accomplished either by increasing the charge or by adding the remaining refrigerant in the hoses into the A/C system.

Refrigerant Weighing Scale

Refrigerant Handling Equipment

Various types of refrigerant machines are available for servicing A/C systems.

Recovery and recycling only. The refrigerant is drawn into a refillable tank. In one design, the refrigerant will be processed through a heat exchanger to remove any oil, then through filters into a storage tank. The other design will draw the refrigerant through a heat exchanger to remove the oil and send the refrigerant to a storage tank. When the storage tank is full, the machine will recycle the entire tank of refrigerant. The machine will be equipped with an oil collection bottle which must be checked to determine how much oil was removed from the A/C system during recovery. The machine will also have a purge mode to remove non-condensables (air) from the recovered refrigerant. The recovery and recycling equipment must meet SAE standards J1990 for R-12 and J2210 for R-134a.

Recovery and Recycling (only) Machine

NOTES:

Recovery, Recycling, and Recharge Machine

Recovery, recycle, and recharge machines. These are the most popular and practical machines available. These machines recover the refrigerant into a refrigerant tank, recycle the refrigerant to remove air, moisture and oil from the refrigerant, evacuate the A/C system with an on-board vacuum pump, and then recharge the A/C system.

New EPA regulations based on SAE standard J2788 went into effect in December 2007. The new standard requires recovery/recycle/recharge machines to recover 95% of the refrigerant system within 30 minutes at 70° F. The machine must measure the amount of refrigerant removed from the system to within one ounce and automatically purge air from the refrigerant, separate oil recovered from the refrigerant and indicate that amount. When charging the A/C system, the machine must charge to within 0.5 ounces of the refrigerant charge. SAE Standard J2788 also states that the machine must monitor filter and vacuum pump oil for replacement, and provide a means to check refrigerant scale calibration. This standard supersedes the old R-134a SAE standard J2210. However, a repair shop may continue to use machines that meet the J2210 standard.

HOSE TOOLS

Hose tool kits include components needed to repair and construct replacement hoses. Crimped fittings and hoses must meet the SAE J2064 standard, so it is important that the correct hose and fittings are used. The correct dies must be used and the ferrule must be crimped properly to the hose and fitting to form a connection that will meet the J2064 standard.

Hose Construction and Repair Tool Kit

NOTES:

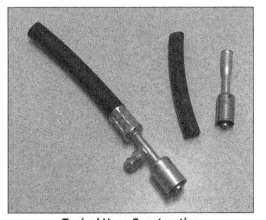

Typical Hose Construction

SYSTEM CLEANING

System flushing may be necessary to remove contaminated oil and debris from the A/C system after a compressor failure. Some system manufacturers do not approve of flushing products for use in the A/C systems, while others approve that the system be flushed with the refrigerant used in the system. Still others approve the use of in-line filters and filter screens when the new components are installed. In-line filters and filter screens are available through various suppliers.

Many late model systems require the condenser to be replaced due to the tiny passages that will become clogged with debris and will not flush out.

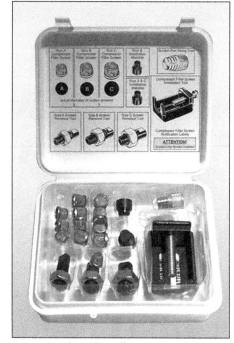

Suction Line Filter Screen Kit

In-line Filter

Flushing equipment will range from stand alone machines,

NOTES:

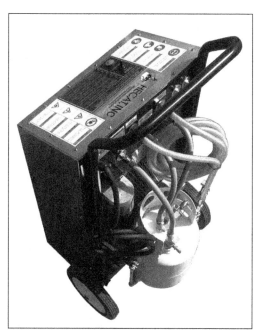

Stand-alone Flushing Machine

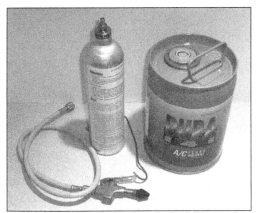

Pressurized Container Equipment

. . . to pressurized containers with adaptors and catch hoses.

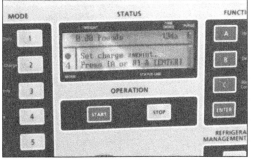

Programmable R/R/R Machine

Some R/R/R machines are capable of flushing and have built in programs to use this feature.

If the vehicle has a new generation condenser, it probably cannot be flushed and must be replaced. Temperature testing can help to determine if the condenser is restricted.

NOTES:

MISCELLANEOUS SERVICE TOOLS

The following items are service tools that are necessary for vehicle specific applications. Many of these tools are available from tool trucks or parts stores as well as the A/C specialty suppliers.

Spring-lock coupling disconnection tools. Many vehicles are equipped with spring-lock fittings which require special tools to disconnect. Kits are available with the various size tools to match the different size fittings.

Spring-lock Coupling Disconnection Tools

Kits are also available to clean the fittings before reassembly to ensure a leak proof seal.

Spring Lock Coupling Cleaning Kit

Orifice tube removal. A special tool is sometimes needed to remove orifice tubes. The kit may include a broken tube remover which is necessary if the orifice tube housing breaks off during an initial removal attempt.

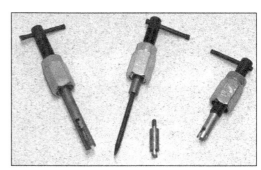
Orifice Tube Removal Tools

NOTES:

Valve Core Tools

Valve core tools. Tools are available to remove and replace service port valve cores. Some allow removal and replacement of the valve core without removing the refrigerant charge.

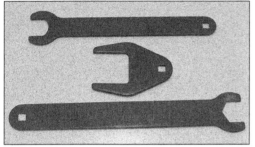

Fan Clutch Tools

Fan clutch. Some viscous fan clutches are threaded directly to the water pump shaft and a special wrench is required to remove and install the clutch assembly.

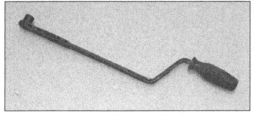

Serpentine Belt Tool

Serpentine belt. Due to limited access in the engine compartment, a special wrench is sometimes needed to release the belt self-tensioner.

Evaporator Cleaner

Evaporator cleaners. Often, molds and fungus will develop on the evaporator core due to high humidity or leaves and pollen entering the plenum. The air flowing from the dash outlets will have a mildew odor that is objectionable to most people. Cleaning kits and aerosol products are available to clean and condition the evaporator core to inhibit further bacterial growth.

NOTES:

NOTES:

NOTES:

Section 7: A/C System Testing and Diagnosis

INTRODUCTION

Although air conditioning systems vary from vehicle to vehicle and system designs vary between manufacturers, following a systematic approach to testing and diagnosis will provide accurate and consistent repairs. Following a step by step process and answering some key questions will help to pinpoint the problem and make the necessary repairs. The step by step process includes the following:

- What are the symptoms?
- What caused the symptoms?
- Confirm the problem.
- Isolate the problem.
- Make the repairs.
- Verify the problem is fixed.

What are the symptoms? Get a complete description of the problem; does the problem happen all the time or only during certain time of day or during certain driving conditions? Get a complete service history. Is this the first time the problem has occurred. Has the vehicle been serviced recently or has it recently been in a collision?

What caused the symptoms? The system should be operated in an attempt to replicate the problem. Operate the A/C system through all settings. Do the outputs change and correspond to the commanded settings? It is possible that the concern may be a normal operating condition? Often the vehicle owner never reads the owner's manual and bases the A/C system's operation on experience with a different vehicle.

Confirm the problem. This involves performing a certain diagnostic procedure to identify the problem. Carry out a visual inspection of the A/C system for leaks, noise and odors. The tests may include control functions, checking for sufficient cooling and overall performance.

Isolate the problem. This may depend on the technician's knowledge of common A/C system failures and component malfunctions. It may also include checking TSBs for updates on repair procedures, and reprogramming on-vehicle electronic modules.

Make the repairs. This involves making necessary adjustments, repairs or component replacement. By performing a complete diagnosis, the correct repair process can be completed.

Verify the repairs. Perform a complete after-repair inspection of the A/C system, operate the controls through all settings, and conduct a final performance test including a temperature drop test.

PRELIMINARY TESTS

Before diagnosing the cause of an A/C system problem, perform the following preliminary checks. These can save time and can help pinpoint the root cause of the problem or expose additional problems that are affecting A/C system operation.

Check the cooling system. When diagnosing A/C system problems, remember that the cooling system can have an impact on A/C system performance. While inspecting the cooling system be sure to check the following items:

Check the Cooling System

• Coolant leaks at the water pump shaft seal, hoses and heat exchangers.

• Pressure cap should be tight and clean.

• Coolant condition and level.

• Check coolant for excessive voltage (electrolysis); 0.3 volts is the maximum allowed. Test coolant only. Do not let the voltmeter probe touch the radiator core or neck.

• Cooling fan(s) operation.

• Loose or missing air dams or fan shrouds.

• Dirty and bent condenser air fins, debris between the condenser and radiator.

• Drive belt condition.

Electrical system. Modern vehicles are electrically dependant and any vehicle system can be affected by a weak battery and low or excessive charging system output. Perform an electrical system output test; be sure to check the following items:

Electrical System Output Test

• Battery should be charged at 12.4 volts minimum, with battery cables clean and tight.

• Alternator output must be within specification.

• Check alternator drive belt and tensioner condition.

NOTES:

Check All Airflow and Temperature Modes for Proper Operation

Air delivery system. Proper airflow, volume and correct temperature change are essential for good A/C system performance. Perform a function test with the vehicle running and check the following items:

- Vacuum reservoir, vacuum lines and fittings (if equipped). Listen for vacuum leaks. If air delivery stays in one mode regardless of mode setting, this can indicate a vacuum leak.

- Operate mode selector. Check to make sure the airflow outlet corresponds to the position selected on the control head. Check vacuum and electrical connections, mode doors, and linkage.

- Move temperature selector. Make sure the temperature output matches the setting on the control head. If temperature does not change, check electrical connection and cable adjustment and temperature door(s) linkage.

- Change blower motor positions. Ensure that the speed change matches setting and air volume matches speed setting. If speed or volume is not correct, check the blower switch, blower resistor, relay(s), blower wheel (squirrel cage) and cabin filter (if equipped).

NOTES:

Air Conditioning System. Inspect the A/C system and check the system for pressure. Check the following:

- Compressor and clutch condition. Look for oil leaks, discolored clutch indicating slippage or compressor seizure, missing hardware and brackets.

- Compressor drive belt. Check for correct tension, glazing, or missing segments.

- Lines and hose assemblies. Check for oil indicating leaks, look for kinks or damage. Check for lines contacting body components or other items which could cause noisy operation.

- Evaporator drain. Check the drain for debris or restrictions. Check the plenum for cracks or damage.

- Condenser. Check for debris in the air fins, bent or damaged air fins, missing air dams or baffles. Check mounting brackets and line for cracks and damage.

- A/C circuit. Check the wiring harness to compressor clutch and control switches for damage and loose connections.

REFRIGERANT CHECKS

After performing the visual checks on the sub-systems and the A/C system, the next step is to check the amount, condition, and type of refrigerant in the A/C system. Connect the low side pressure gauge to verify that there is pressure in the system. If there is at least 50 psi pressure in the system, the following tests can be performed:

Sealant Detection. Sealer has become the latest "quick fix" for A/C systems. Sale of R-134a refrigerant is not restricted to certified technicians. Consumers have access not only to R-134a but a variety of chemicals that can be detrimental to the A/C system and service equipment. Many of the products marketed as sealants for leaking systems, or A/C system "enhancers" may have sealant included with oil. Use of the sealer may void warranties regardless of component supplier or equipment manufacturer.

A sealer tester kit will determine if sealer is in the system by using a test orifice and flow meter. The test orifice is wetted with water and attached to the high side of the A/C system. A section of rubber hose is connected from the orifice to a flow meter. The A/C system is operated for 10 minutes, and then shut off. The test pieces are attached to the high-pressure side of the system and the ball in the flow meter is marked. After three minutes, the position of the ball is checked. If the ball has fallen below the check point, the system contains sealer.

NOTES:

Refrigerant identification. Every vehicle that comes in for A/C service should have an identifier connected to determine the condition of the refrigerant as well as the type of refrigerant in the system. Two percent is the maximum amount of air that can be in the system or source tank. Unusual readings such as multiple refrigerants present in the system can be an indication of the presence of a blend. New virgin tanks should be checked as well. Some new tanks have been reported to have as much as 5% air or more.

Leak detection. A refrigerant leak test should be performed on an A/C system whenever a performance problem such as poor cooling is encountered, or there are indications of leaks at components and fittings. A leak test should be performed after any service operation where connections were opened or a component was replaced. The two preferred methods of leak testing are with an electronic leak detector or using a UV lamp with fluorescent trace dye.

Electronic leak detectors. When using electronic leak detectors, the SAE J1628 standard should be followed:

- Engine is turned off.
- The A/C system must have a minimum of 50 psi static pressure with a minimum ambient air temperature of 60°F.
- Visually trace the entire A/C system, look for signs of oil leaks, damage or corrosion on lines, hoses, fittings and components. Wipe off the area to be checked with a clean shop towel before checking for a leak.
- Follow the refrigerant system in one direction completely around the entire system so no lines or components are missed.
- Move the test probe completely around the area being tested, with the probe moving at a rate that does not exceed one inch per second. The probe must be held no farther than 1/4" from the surface being tested.
- When a leak is found, blow compressed air around the area to displace any refrigerant, move the test probe to fresh air and reset, then repeat the test to confirm the leak.
- **Testing for Evaporator Leaks.** With the A/C system operating, turn on the blower motor to maximum speed for a minimum of 15 seconds. Turn off the blower motor and wait 10 minutes. Either remove the resistor block and insert the test probe into the evaporator case or insert the test probe into the evaporator case drain. Be sure the drain opening is dry to prevent damage to the testing probe. If neither is possible, try to gain access to the evaporator some other way.

Fluorescent trace dyes. Trace dye is a colored liquid that mixes with the refrigerant oil and will leak out of the system along with the refrigerant and oil at a leak point.

- Add the proper amount of dye to the A/C system per the dye manufacturer's instructions. **Attention: Many manufacturers install dye at the factory when the vehicle is built. Always check service information and the refrigerant label on the vehicle before installing dye.**

- Operate the A/C system for 10-15 minutes to circulate the dye throughout the system. Small leaks may take several days to appear and if the oil never reaches the leak point, no visual indications will be seen.

- Shine the UV lamp on the A/C system and look for the dye, which is usually green or yellow. **Attention: Always use the eyewear that is part of the dye test kit. The glasses will protect your eyes from the ultraviolet lamp and enhance the color of the dye, which helps to find small leaks.**

- Wipe the inside of the evaporator drain tube with a cotton swab. Hold the swab under the UV lamp. Any dye on the swab indicates an evaporator core leak.

- Clean any dye off the components after repairs to prevent a false reading during future testing.

NOTES:

Using R/R/R Machine Gauges to Conduct Performance Test

Performance Test Gauge Readings

Performance Test. This test provides information about the air conditioning system's operating efficiency. The A/C system high-side and low-side pressures are measured and the discharge temperature in the passenger compartment is measured. Equipment needed for this test is:

• Manifold gauges, either a stand-alone set or ones that are part of a recovery, recycling, and recharging machine.

• A thermometer and a device to control engine RPM.

The performance test is a vital procedure that reveals the state of health of the A/C system. It is important that the specific vehicle setup be followed to get valid data on the A/C system's operation. In this age of multiple compressor designs and various control valves, the test standard will vary with model and make. If the correct procedure is not followed, misdiagnosis can lead to the wrong parts being replaced and the condition the vehicle came in for will still exist.

• Service information is very critical and must be kept updated. Make sure to check the latest updates and TSBs.

• Set vehicle to recommended parameters. This setup will vary depending on the type of compressor and expansion device (orifice tube or thermostatic expansion valve).

• One size does not fit all! Operating the engine at the wrong RPM, setting the dash controls to the wrong position, or having the doors, windows and the hood in the wrong position will result in the pressure and temperature readings being inaccurate, which can lead to misdiagnosis.

• Ambient temperature and humidity readings are critical. Some A/C systems must be tested with a minimum ambient temperature of 60° F, while on others, the minimum ambient temperature is 70° F. High humidity can increase the pressures and temperatures from the A/C system. Many A/C performance charts will provide the pressure and temperature values under various ambient temperature and humidity conditions.

Temperature test. Manufacturers have phased in critical charge systems, which means less refrigerant is used. Service equipment that does not meet the J2788 standard will often mis-charge a system. Component temperature testing is an effective way of confirming the charge level and checking the performance of each component.

Heat load is very important for temperature testing to be successful. If ambient temperature is too low, the readings will not be in the correct range, and this could lead to misdiagnosis. As with any repair or diagnostic procedure, proper setup and test conditions are needed.

Temperature testing does not replace performance testing, but it does confirm refrigerant charge and helps find restrictions in lines and components.

Both the performance and temperature tests are necessary to achieve a complete system check. Although the tests are similar, they do have important differences. The performance test is used to ensure that the system is meeting its original design criteria. This includes the compressor's ability to achieve specific suction and discharge pressures at various heat load conditions. Temperature testing places the system in the worst case situation (maximum load) to see if there are any hidden problems or out of range components, as well as checking for the correct charge level.

NOTES:

As shown below, the vehicle setup differs for each type of test. During the performance test, vehicle setup is determined by system design. Results are reflected in gauge pressures and duct temperature. The temperature test setup is the same for all system designs, and the target is temperature change at the heat exchangers and the ambient to duct temperature difference. Utilizing both tests will measure the true performance of an A/C system.

TEST SETUPS	
Temperature Test	**Performance Test**
Vehicle at operating temperature	Vehicle at operating temperature
Engine at idle	Engine RPM: Set to specs
All doors open	Doors: Set to specs
A/C Max Cold	A/C: Set to specs
Blower speed high	Blower speed: Set to specs
Measure Temperature Difference	**Measure Low and High Pressures**
Condenser inlet to outlet	Measure duct temperature
Evaporator inlet to outlet	
Ambient/duct	

Temperature Test Target Ranges

Based on multiple vehicle studies, the values listed on the next page are consistent for orifice tube equipped vehicles when the vehicle is tested following the recommended setup: engine idling at normal operating temperature, all doors open, A/C controls in the maximum/recirculation air selection, full cold for the temperature setting, and maximum blower speed. When performing temperature testing on TXV equipped vehicles, evaporator inlet to outlet testing will not be available. Use only the condenser and ambient-to-duct values.

NOTES:

Expected Temperature Difference with Correct Refrigerant Charge

Condenser inlet to outlet temperature difference:

    20° F minimum

    50° F maximum

Evaporator inlet to outlet temperature range:

    Plus or minus 5° F

    0° F difference ideal

Duct air to ambient air:

    30° F minimum difference

EXAMPLE OF A TYPICAL A/C PERFORMANCE CHART

Ambient Air Temperature	Humidity	Low Side Pressure	High Side Pressure	Center Duct Discharge Temperature
55 – 65° F	0 – 100%	25 – 30 psi	49 – 123 psi	45° F
66 – 75° F	40% or Less	25 – 31 psi	62 – 135 psi	43° F
66 – 75° F	Over 40%	25 – 37 psi	83 – 85 psi	48° F
76 – 85° F	35% or Less	25 – 37 psi	147 – 205 psi	42° F
76 – 85° F	35 – 60%	26 – 38 psi	120 – 171 psi	50° F
86 – 95° F	30% or Less	28 – 43 psi	146 – 205 psi	54° F
86 – 95° F	30 – 50%	30 – 44 psi	153 – 209 psi	55° F
86 – 95° F	Over 50%	32 – 47 psi	160 – 213 psi	58° F
96 – 105° F	20% or Less	35 – 47 psi	190 – 246 psi	61° F
96 – 105° F	20 – 40 %	36 – 50 psi	190 – 230 psi	61° F
96 – 105° F	Over 40%	37 – 52 psi	196 – 246 psi	61° F
106 – 115° F	20% or Less	42 – 55 psi	238 – 283 psi	62° F
106 – 115° F	Over 20%	43 – 55 psi	235 – 280 psi	66° F

NOTES:

Gauge Readings

If the A/C system pressures and duct temperature do not meet the performance chart ranges, record the high- and low-pressure gauge readings and compare them to the following examples. Ambient temperature, humidity, and vehicle color can affect system performance. The following examples suggest problems that could be present at the given gauge readings.

LOW SIDE AND HIGH SIDE NORMAL

Possible causes:

- Air delivery problem – check for blend door adjustment/damage.
- A/C control problem – check for calibration, check voltage/or vacuum sources.

Low Side and High Side Normal

LOW SIDE AND HIGH SIDE BOTH LOW

Possible causes:

- Low refrigerant charge.
- TXV/orifice tube inlet restriction.

Low Side and High Side Low

NOTES:

LOW SIDE AND HIGH SIDE BOTH HIGH

Possible causes:

- Air in the system.
- Refrigerant or oil overcharge.
- Air flow restriction through condenser.
- Faulty expansion valve or orifice tube – O-rings not sealing.

Low Side and High Side High

LOW SIDE HIGH AND HIGH SIDE LOW

Possible causes:

- Internal compressor failure.

Low Side High and High Side Low

Temperature Testing. When the A/C system fails to meet the performance standard, temperature testing will provide additional information to help find the root cause. With the vehicle set up for temperature testing, the diagram on the next page shows the various test points. The vehicle setup is engine idling at normal operating temperature, full cold position, maximum blower speed, all the doors open, ambient temperature at 70° F minimum.

NOTES:

Temperature Testing an Orifice Tube System

Inlet

Condenser

Ambient

Low Pressure

Compressor

Accumulator

Outlet

Outlet

Evaporator

High Pressure

Duct →

Orifice Tube

Inlet

Temperature Test Check Points (OT System)

The callouts at the condenser and evaporator show the locations where the temperature readings should be taken to get the expected results.

• When testing at the condenser, attach the test probes to the condenser inlet and outlet pipes as close to the condenser core as possible.

• When testing at the evaporator, attach the test probes to the evaporator inlet and outlet pipes as close to the evaporator core as possible.

• The duct temperature reading should be taken at the vent closest to the evaporator.

• Hoses and lines should have a 4° F maximum difference from end to end.

• Muffler assemblies should have a maximum of 10° F drop from the inlet side to the outlet side.

NOTES:

Temperature Testing a Thermostatic Expansion Valve System

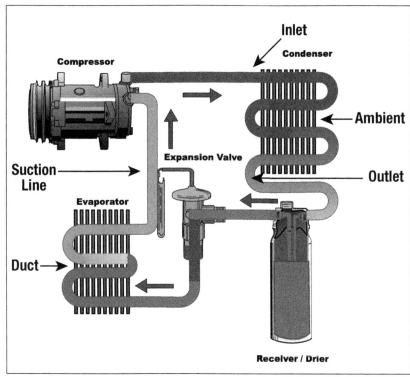

Temperature Test Check Points (TXV System)

Above are the test points when performing a temperature test on a TXV system. The two main checks are condenser inlet and outlet and ambient-to-duct. With TXV systems, the condenser temperature test is telling of the state of charge in the system.

NOTES:

Temperature Test Diagnostic Readings. The following charts indicate causes if the temperature test readings are out of range.

CONDENSER TEMPERATURE READINGS OUT OF RANGE	
Inlet to outlet temperature more than 50° F	**Inlet to outlet temperature less than 20° F**
System undercharged	System overcharged
Excessive air in system	• Condenser air fins plugged
Condenser tubes plugged	Airflow problems:
	• Cooling fans not working properly
	• Debris between condenser and radiator

EVAPORATOR TEMPERATURE READINGS OUT OF RANGE (Orifice tube system)	
Outlet pipe is more than 5° F warmer than the inlet pipe	**Outlet pipe is more than 5° F colder than the inlet pipe**
System undercharged	System overcharged
Excessive oil charge	Orifice tube O-ring not sealing
Restricted orifice tube	

AMBIENT TO DUCT TEMPERATURE READINGS OUT OF RANGE (Ambient-to-duct temperature less than a 30° F difference)	
System charge may not be correct	
Blend door faulty	
Evaporator internal restrictions	
Excessive oil in system	
Air in system	
Recirc/outside air door faulty	
Evaporator air fins plugged	

NOTES:

Sources that cause poor A/C system performance

- Leaks (which lead to an undercharged system) – always leak test the entire A/C system.
- Air in the A/C system – use refrigerant analyzer, recover refrigerant and purge air.
- Excessive pressure and temperature – check condenser airflow and cooling system. Also possible overcharge.
- Lines or hoses restricted – check for internal hose barrier delamination.
- Excessive oil in system – replace receiver/drier or accumulator, flush system and add proper amount.
- Non-approved additives – check for sealant and "enhancers."
- Contamination:
  - *Air* – increases pressures.
  - *Moisture* – causes TXVs to freeze and causes corrosion.
  - *Debris* – rubber and metal shavings clog and damage components.
  - *Residual cleaning solvents* – break down oil and reduce lubrication.
  - *Wrong oil* – reduces lubrication.

NOTES:

A/C COMPONENT MALFUNCTIONS

A/C component malfunctions can occur due to low refrigerant charge, lack of lubrication, or by any of the items listed as sources that cause poor A/C performance. The following descriptions list malfunctions that can occur with each of the A/C system components.

Compressor. Malfunctions will include noise, seizure, leaking, and low suction or discharge pressure.

Noise can be caused by loose or missing hardware or caused by internal compressor damage including broken reed plates, worn bearings, piston damage, etc.

Seizure can be caused by refrigerant leaks, restrictions in the system or control device malfunction. All of these can cause reduced or no lubricant flow through the compressor.

Leaking can occur at the shaft seal, center joints, or head assembly.

Compressor Malfunctions

High suction and low discharge pressures can be caused by control valve failure on variable displacement designs, damaged pistons or reed valves, or worn out parts.

*High Suction, Low Discharge
Pressure Readings*

NOTES:

Condenser problems are either caused by leaks, internal or external restrictions, or physical damage.

Leaks can be caused by corrosion from road salt and other environmental pollutants. Leaks can also be caused by loose or broken mounting hardware which allows the condenser body or inlet and outlet tubes to rub against other items.

Restrictions may be internal or external. Internal restrictions may be the result of debris from another failed component that clogs the small internal passageways. Or the condenser may corrode internally due to moisture in the system. External restrictions include dirt or insects clogging the air fins or bent air fins.

Damage can be caused by road debris such as rocks and stones, or, of course, a collision.

Condenser

Orifice tube problems may include:

• The inlet screen on the OT being clogged or restricted; the OT is the main filter in an orifice tube system. It should be inspected whenever the A/C system is opened.

• The OT may be installed backwards. The small end of the OT must face toward the evaporator core.

• The wrong size OT may have been installed. Orifice tubes are sized for the system and are color coded by size.

• The OT O-rings may not properly seal inside the line.

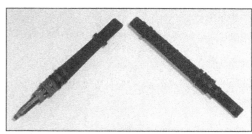
Clogged Orifice Tubes

NOTES:

_____

_____

_____

_____

_____

_____

_____

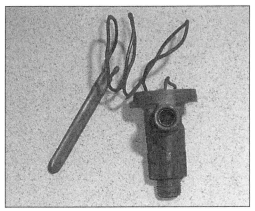

Clogged Thermostatic Expansion Valve

Thermostatic expansion valve problems may include:

- A clogged inlet.
- The sensing bulb may lose its refrigerant charge, or the sensing bulb may not be positioned correctly on the evaporator outlet.
- The wrong TXV may have been installed which can cause the evaporator to freeze or not get cold enough.
- The push rod(s) in the TXV may corrode and stick. This will cause the TXV to either flood or starve the evaporator.

The TXV can be tested by freezing the sensing diaphragm. The low-side pressure should drop to 0 psi or into a vacuum when the sensing diaphragm is chilled. As the TXV warms up, the low-side pressure should stabilize at normal.

Clogged Evaporator

Evaporator problems include poor cooling due to debris plugging the air fins of the core, leaks caused by corrosion, or internal baffles collapsing or coming loose causing a blockage. Other evaporator related problems might include a plugged plenum condensate drain or restricted cabin filter (if equipped).

NOTES:

Receiver/driers and accumulators rarely fail themselves. When a failure does occur with one of these components, it is usually due either to clogging from some type of debris in the A/C system, or that the desiccant has disintegrated. This will cause loss of desiccant effectiveness, and could possibly cause clogging in other system components (such as a TXV or orifice tube).

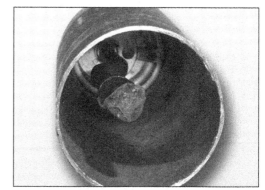

Clogged Receiver/Drier

Refrigerant line restriction problems include inner liners collapsing, bent or kinked lines, or internal filters clogging. The best way to check lines and hoses, including mufflers, is temperature testing. The maximum temperature drop on a straight line is 4° F. If the line has a muffler, the maximum temperature drop is 10° F.

Restricted Refrigerant Line

Insufficient refrigerant charge. Any loss of refrigerant will reduce the system's ability to cool and dehumidify the passenger compartment. The reduced charge will also affect compressor lubrication. The refrigerant holds the oil in suspension. If the refrigerant level is too low, the compressor may fail.

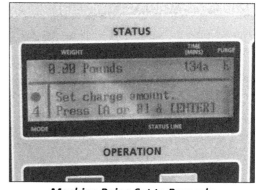

Machine Being Set to Properly Recharge a System

NOTES:

Scan for Compressor Control System Problems

Compressor controls. If the compressor clutch will not engage or the evaporator freezes, or the cooling fans do not operate properly, the problem could be related to the A/C system electrical controls or the vehicle's engine management systems. Scan tools, digital meters and complete vehicle service information will be required to address these issues.

ACCESSING A/C SYSTEM SERVICE INFORMATION

The A/C system has become an integral part of the vehicle. It may be necessary to access the manufacturers' websites to view A/C system component details, system operation, DTCs, wiring diagrams and TSBs. The OEM sites will provide data based on platform and by VIN.

NOTES:

VIN:	3GNDA33P57S623360
Controller:	ECM Engine Control Module

Calibration History for: **Main Operating System**

Part Number	CVN	Bulletin #	Description
12610013	000074F1	-	Main Operating System

Calibration History for: **System**

Part Number	CVN	Bulletin #	Description
12618356	0000B26F	-	System

Calibration History for: **Fuel system**

Part Number	CVN	Bulletin #	Description
12614070	00006106	-	New calibration with diagnostic enhancements for DTCs P0461.
12600874	000074D7	-	Fuel System

Calibration History for: **Speedometer**

Part Number	CVN	Bulletin #	Description
12600877	000033B7	-	Speedometer

Calibration History for: **Engine diagnostic**

Part		Bulletin	

GM Vehicle Calibration Information

National Automotive Service Task Force

News   About NASTF   Mission   Logo Use   Directory   Participant Login   Events   Contact Us

Vehicle Security Information

Information Requests

OEM Service Websites

Additional Information Sources

Information Access Charges

Service Information Matrix

Reprogramming Information

Tools Matrix

Training Matrix

Collision Matrix

Committees

NASTF General Meetings

OEM Service Websites

Acura – http://www.ServiceExpress.Honda.com

Aston Martin - www.astonmartintechinfo.com/home

Audi – https://erwin.audiusa.com

Bentley – http://www.bentleytechinfo.com

BMW – http://www.bmwtechinfo.com

Chrysler/Dodge/Eagle/Jeep/Plymouth – http://www.techauthority.com

Ferrari - www.ferraritechinfo.com

Ford/Lincoln/Mercury – http://www.motorcraftservice.com

General Motors –
Buick/Cadillac/Chevrolet/Geo/GMC/Hummer/Oldsmobile/Pontiac/Saturn –
http://www.gmtechinfo.com

Honda – http://www.ServiceExpress.Honda.com

Hyundai – http://www.hmaservice.com or http://www.hyundaitechinfo.com

Infiniti – http://www.infiniti-techinfo.com

Isuzu – http://www.isuzutechinfo.com (no key code access)

Jaguar – http://www.jaguartechinfo.com

Kia – http://www.kiatechinfo.com

Land Rover – http://www.landrovertechinfo.com

Lexus – http://techinfo.lexus.com

Maserati - www.maseratitechinfo.com

Mazda – www.mazdaserviceinfo.com

Mercedes Benz – http://www.startekinfo.com

Mini – http://www.minitechinfo.com

Mitsubishi – http://www.mitsubishitechinfo.com

Nissan – http://www.nissan-techinfo.com

Porsche – https://techinfo2.porsche.com/PAGInfosystem/VFModuleManager?Type=GVOStart

Rolls Royce - http://www.rrtis.com

Saab – http://www.saabtechinfo.com

Smart - http://owners.smartusa.com/Subscription_Plans.aspx

Subaru – http://techinfo.subaru.com

Suzuki – http://suzukipitstopplus.com

Toyota/Scion – http://techinfo.toyota.com

Volkswagen – https://erwin.vw.com

Volvo – http://www.volvotechinfo.com

The NASTF Website Provides Links to almost All OEM Service Information

In addition to the OEM sites, aftermarket websites are available. Companies like Mitchell and ALLDATA provide service information on a subscription basis.

NOTES:

Section 8: A/C System Service and Repair

INTRODUCTION

Once the vehicle has been diagnosed, the next step will be to make the necessary repairs. This section will cover:

- Refrigerant recovery
- System flushing and filtering
- Component replacement
- Oil replacement
- Evacuation
- System recharge
- After repairs leak testing
- Final performance and temperature testing.

Refrigerant Recovery. As required by law, the refrigerant in the A/C system must be recovered. **Attention:** Follow the operator's manual for setup, operation and maintenance for R/R/R machines.

R/R/R Machine

NOTES:

Refrigerant Recovery and Recycling Procedures
Before You Begin ...

ENSURE SYSTEM INTEGRITY

Perform a visual inspection to spot obvious problems.

CHECK FOR PRESSURE IN THE SYSTEM

It would make no sense to attempt refrigerant recovery from a system that contains no refrigerant. Because of this, always check to see if the system has pressure by installing a pressure gauge on a system service port before starting a recovery process.

If a system contains no pressure, it is a safe assumption that the refrigerant has leaked out, and one of your first steps should be trying to track down a leak or leaks in the system.

Perform a Visual Inspection

THE EFFECT OF SYSTEM DESIGN ON THE REFRIGERANT RECOVERY PROCESS

When refrigerant is removed from the system, the lowering of pressure results in some of the system components becoming cooler. This cooling effect can make complete refrigerant removal in a short period of time more difficult.

To remove as much of the refrigerant as possible during the recovery process, systems equipped with orifice tubes and accumulators may require more time than systems equipped with expansion valves and receiver/driers. This is mainly because of the design differences between accumulators and receiver/driers (being larger than receiver/driers, accumulators hold more refrigerant and oil than do receiver/driers).

During the recovery process, as the system is drawn into a vacuum, and pressure in the accumulator is lowered, the accumulator becomes very cold, with external frost sometimes visible on the accumulator. This makes it more difficult to extract remaining refrigerant from it.

NOTES:

Heating an Accumulator During Refrigerant Recovery

Heating the accumulator with a device such as a hair dryer or electric heating pad will raise the pressure in the accumulator and reduce the amount of time necessary for refrigerant removal.

When recovering refrigerant from any mobile A/C system, continue the recovery process until the system has been reduced from a pressure to a vacuum. At this point, pause operation of the recovery machine for five minutes, and check A/C system pressure. If pressure has risen above vacuum, additional recovery is required to remove remaining refrigerant. Repeat the recovery process until the vacuum remains stable, without rising, for two minutes.

Most modern recovery/recycling machines have a built-in five-minute wait period after the system is first drawn into a vacuum, and if a rise in system pressure is sensed, will automatically repeat the recovery process until the system will remain at a stable vacuum.

Cautions:

- At no time should an open flame torch be used to heat the accumulator.

- All refrigerant must be removed before opening any of the system's connections.

MORE COMPLETE REFRIGERANT RECOVERY

To recover as much refrigerant as possible, warm up the system's underhood components with engine and, as already mentioned, apply external heat to the accumulator (if the system has one).

There are differences in the percentage of refrigerant that's recovered using best techniques versus shortcuts. A single "pull" on a cool morning might remove 60% of the charge, whereas a careful procedure, using heat to promote outgassing, might remove the over 90% that is necessary for accurate service.

Any refrigerant not removed from a system during recovery remains in it and could cause potential problems. If you don't physically apply heat to the system components (especially accumulators) before you start a recovery process, you should first run the engine up to operating temperature, so at least some heat will transfer to the A/C components.

What happens to the refrigerant you didn't get out of the system during recovery?

ENGINE PRE-HEAT FOR REFRIGERANT REMOVAL PROCEDURE

The following procedure will aid in refrigerant removal when the work area is cool and J2210 and J1732 recovery equipment is being used. In general if the work area is warmer than 90° F (32° C) this procedure is not required.

Recovery equipment certified to J2788 and J2810 does not require this pre-warming procedure.

Removal Procedure

1. A/C System Controls

   ◇ Compressor clutch off
   - Turn clutch off or remove electrical connection

   ◇ Set panel system controls
   - Outside air (not max)
   - High fan speed
   - Airflow panel outlets
   - ATC Systems: Set temperature mid range
     ○ Check to make sure system is on outside air, drawing air from vehicle cowl air inlet area

2. Vehicle hood open to allow warm engine air to enter cowl inlet to A/C system

   ◇ Operate engine idle condition

   - Neutral (park) with parking brake applied
   - Depending upon engine compartment temperature:
     ○ Run engine to warm up A/C system components for 15 minutes

   ◇ After idling engine for 15 minutes (hot condition)

   - Stop engine and then turn ignition to on position allowing operation of:
     ○ A/C fan high; system on Outside air
     ○ When applicable – Operation of electric engine cooling fan to circulate air in engine compartment
     ○ Do not change any control or conditions listed in steps 1 and 2 above
     ○ Start refrigerant recovery process

   ◇ When refrigerant recovery is completed, including the required 5 minute recheck for system pressure (system refrigerant out gassing), shut vehicle and equipment off.

NOTES:

NOTES:

If the system is opened, the remaining refrigerant will be vented to the atmosphere and you have discarded perfectly good, reusable refrigerant.

If your vacuum pump isn't performing properly – not performing a deep vacuum – or in the interest of saving time – you shortcut performing a deep vacuum, you could end up leaving refrigerant in the system.

If you then recharge the system to specification, you will end up with an overcharge. This costs you money, because you're using more refrigerant than necessary, and the more jobs you do this way, the more money you're losing.

Use of SAE J2788 equipment will assure improved refrigerant recovery during service.

IMPROPERLY RECYCLED REFRIGERANT

It is important to make sure that recycled refrigerant does not contain air (non-condensable gas) in excess of allowable amounts. If recycled refrigerant contains too much air, high system operating pressure will occur and pressure operated refrigerant controls will have a different control set point. This will result in loss of air conditioning performance and possible system damage.

Properly operating recovery/recycling equipment will remove excess air. Many newer R/R machines have an automatic air purge feature which, if working properly, should assure that its recycled refrigerant will not contain excessive levels of air. However, many older R/R machines require a manual air purge operation.

Make sure you understand which type of air purge feature your machine has and follow its manufacturer's instructions to assure that proper air purging is taking place.

SYSTEM LUBRICANTS AND REFRIGERANT RECOVERY

Recovery-only and recovery/recycling equipment will separate the lubricant during the refrigerant recovery process, so properly recycled refrigerant will not contain too much lubricant.

In general, recovery equipment will remove very little, if any, lubricant from a system. It is a design requirement of the equipment that the amount of lubricant removed during recovery must be measurable. This is usually (but not always) indicated by removed oil being collected in a transparent graduated container.

If a large quantity of lubricant was removed during recovery, the A/C system probably had a lubricant overcharge.

The recovery machine's oil recovery reservoir should be emptied before each recovery operation, then checked when recovery is completed to see how much (if any) oil was removed from the system during recovery. If oil was removed, that same quantity of fresh new oil of the type the system requires must be reinstalled in the system before it is put back into operation.

Lubricant removed during recovery must not be reused in the system. Used lubricant should be disposed of in accordance with federal, state and local requirements. (Visit *www.ecarcenter.org/ ecartour.html* for more information on specific disposal requirements).

Typical R/R Machine Oil Recovery Reservoir

System Flushing is used to remove contaminated refrigerant oil and debris from the components. Evaporators, lines without mufflers, and some condensers may be flushed. Most parallel flow condensers, and all compressors, orifice tubes, TXVs, mufflers, and receiver/driers must not be flushed, and must be replaced if they contain debris.

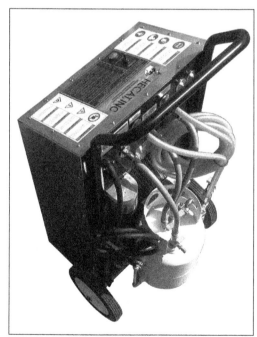

System Flushing Machine

METHODS OF FLUSHING

Refrigerant

- Refrigerant flushing uses liquid refrigerant to remove the oil and possibly some debris.
- Refrigerant will not damage components, and can be recycled.
- Will not harm the A/C system.

Flushing Solvents

- Require special equipment.
- Flushing solvent must be completely removed from system.
- Flush may react with A/C refrigerant and oil if not properly and completely removed.
- Requires proper disposal.
- Not approved by most OEMs.

Non-approved Flushing Agents

- Air
- Water
- Gasoline
- Paint thinner
- Mineral spirits
- Brake cleaner

In-Line Filter

Filters in Place of, or in Addition to, Flushing

- Added system protection.
- May be used in place of flushing.
- May require replacement after initial operation of the A/C system (filter may quickly clog with debris).

NOTES:

COMPONENT REPLACEMENT

When a failed component is replaced, in addition to following the instructions supplied with the replacement component, and following the procedures in the service information, several other steps must be followed to ensure that the repair is performed properly and completely.

• Replace receiver/drier or accumulator.

• Replace restricted orifice tube (or liquid line if it contains a non-removeable orifice tube).

• Inspect/replace TXV.

• Flush the system (if known to contain debris, contaminated oil, or too much oil).

• Properly evacuate the system.

• Add the correct type and amount of oil.

• Add the correct amount of refrigerant.

Compressors

In addition to the listed steps, the following steps are necessary during compressor replacement.

• Check clutch air gap.

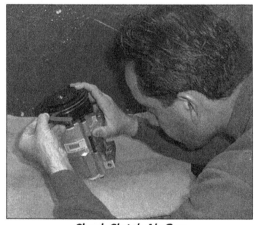

Check Clutch Air Gap

NOTES:

Hand-turn Clutch Hub

• Hand-turn the compressor drive plate hub a minimum of 10 rotations to clear oil from compressor.

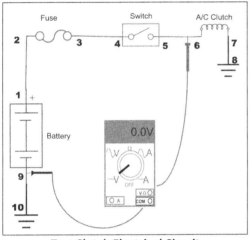

Test Clutch Electrical Circuit

• Test the clutch electrical circuit.
  ▪ The power side should be within one volt of vehicle charging system voltage; the ground side should not show a voltage drop of any more than 0.2 volts (200 millivolts).

Lap the Clutch Assembly

• Burnish the clutch assembly to "break in" its friction surfaces.
  ▪ Run the engine at 2500 rpm.
  ▪ Cycle the compressor clutch; on one second/off two seconds.
  ▪ Repeat a minimum of 25 times.

OIL REPLACEMENT

During normal A/C system operation, a small amount of lubricating oil circulates and is distributed throughout the various components. R-12 refrigerant systems use mineral oil, while R-134a systems use PAG oil. However, hybrid vehicles with electric motor-driven compressors, use **SPECIAL** POE oils.

The type of compressor usually determines the total amount of oil in the system. The amount is usually between 6 and 10 ounces. Always check the service information for the vehicle and the compressor found on the A/C system.

Compressor Suppliers' Oil Policy

Compressor may be shipped:

• Without oil.

• With some oil.

• With a full charge of oil.

• Always check the instructions.

OIL REQUIREMENTS FOR INDIVIDUAL COMPONENTS

Whenever an individual component is replaced, oil must be added to the system to keep the oil level balanced and to ensure that the compressor will stay lubricated. Following is the recommended amount for each component:

Compressors

• Add the same amount that was drained from the old compressor.

• If the amount of oil drained was less than 3 ounces, replace 3 ounces.

• If the amount of oil drained was more than 5 ounces, replace with 5 ounces.

• Some compressors will have a drain plug.

• Refer to the service information for correct levels.

Preparing for Compressor Oil Balancing

Evaporator Core

• Plate-and-fin design, add 3 ounces of oil.

• Tube-and-fin design, add 2 ounces.

• Always check service information.

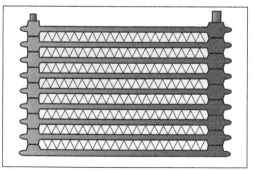

Evaporator Core

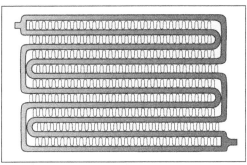

Condenser

Condensers

- 1 ounce

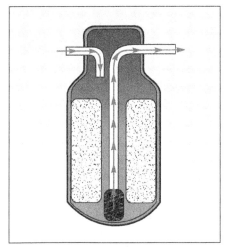

Receiver/Drier

Receiver/Driers

- 2 ounces

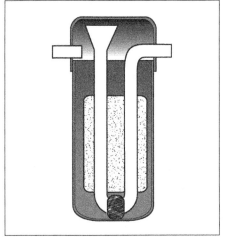

Accumulator/Drier

Accumulator/Driers

- 3 ounces

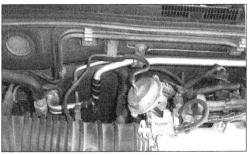

Lines and Hoses

Lines and Hoses

- 0.5 ounce

O-RINGS, GASKETS AND SEALS

Any fitting or connection that has been opened or disturbed must have its sealing component replaced. O-rings should be lubricated with mineral oil. Gaskets and sealing washers are installed dry. The connection must be torqued to the correct value to prevent leaks. If the connection is a spring-lock design, the O-rings and garter springs must be replaced. The fitting should be cleaned with a brass brush or crocus cloth before assembly.

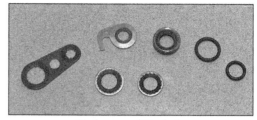

O-rings and Gaskets

RECEIVER/DRIER OR ACCUMULATOR/DRIER

These components are installed last to keep moisture from saturating the desiccant.

Receiver/Drier and Accumulator

EVACUATION

Evacuating the A/C system removes air, residual refrigerant, possibly some moisture, and also possibly residual flush solvent from the system. Evacuate the system to 29.5 inches of mercury for at least 30 minutes on a single evaporator system, and at least 60 minutes on a dual evaporator system. (Evacuation time may possibly be shortened if a J2788 spec. machine was used to recover the refrigerant.) Using a micron gauge will provide a more accurate reading of how deep a vacuum has been drawn. A reading of 500 microns or less indicates that a deep vacuum has been reached.

Any time the system is opened for repairs or if the system has lost all the refrigerant charge, the system must be evacuated. Vacuum pumps are available as stand-alone tools to be used with manifold gauge sets or they may be built into a R/R/R machine.

Begin the evacuation process by connecting the manifold gauges to the A/C system. If a manifold gauge set is used, the center hose attaches to the vacuum pump. R/R/R machines have internal lines that connect the service hoses to the vacuum pump. Start the vacuum pump, then open the low-side hand valve. The low side gauge will begin to drop into a vacuum. Watch the high side

Stand-alone Vacuum Pump

Draw A/C System into Vacuum

Gauges Showing Vacuum

gauge, and when the high-side gauge needle begins to drop into a vacuum, this indicates that there are no restrictions in the A/C system.

Open the high side service valve. Continue to evacuate for 10 minutes. The low side gauge should be reading at least 28 inches of vacuum at sea level. If the vacuum level is 20 to 22 inches of vacuum at sea level, the system may have a leak. Stop evacuation, add enough refrigerant to achieve 50 psi and leak check the system with an electronic leak detector. If a 28 inch or deeper vacuum is reached, close both gauge hand valves.

The valve gauge reading must not rise more than 1 inch after standing for 5 minutes. If the vacuum holds, continue the evacuation process.

Altitude will affect the vacuum readings; for every 1,000 feet of elevation, the vacuum reading will be 1 inch lower than at sea level.

Changing the vacuum pump oil, as its manufacturer recommends, will keep the pump in good working order and will help the pump to reach maximum vacuum.

NOTES:

SYSTEM CHARGING

Recharging the system to the proper level is one of the most important and critical A/C service procedures. Efficient operation and satisfactory A/C performance depends on the correct amount of refrigerant in the system. The effects of the wrong charge level range from poor cooling to compressor failure.

System undercharge will result in poor cooling due to the lack of enough refrigerant to absorb heat. If only slightly undercharged, the system may cool well under mild conditions. An undercharge will cause clutch cycling systems to cycle the compressor clutch more often than normal. However, the worst condition that can result from an undercharge is poor or no oil circulation, which can lead to compressor failure.

System overcharge will result in poor cooling due to a high liquid level in the condenser. During normal A/C operation, a condenser contains two-thirds vapor and one-third liquid. If this ratio is changed, latent heat in the refrigerant will not be released to the outside air. Refrigerant controls may not function properly and the compressor or compressor clutch may fail. An overcharge can cause higher than normal gauge readings, and noisy compressor operation.

Charge tolerance. Modern A/C systems may contain as little as 12 ounces of refrigerant. Any variation from the correct level will cause the system to cool poorly and eventually fail. Always check the refrigerant label on the vehicle or service information for the correct charge levels and any changes that the manufacturer may have made to the A/C system capacity to address performance issues.

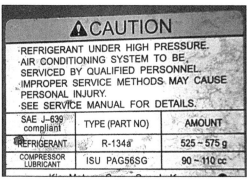

⚠ CAUTION		
REFRIGERANT UNDER HIGH PRESSURE. AIR CONDITIONING SYSTEM TO BE SERVICED BY QUALIFIED PERSONNEL. IMPROPER SERVICE METHODS MAY CAUSE PERSONAL INJURY. SEE SERVICE MANUAL FOR DETAILS.		
SAE J–639 compliant	TYPE (PART NO)	AMOUNT
REFRIGERANT	R-134a	525 ~ 575 g
COMPRESSOR LUBRICANT	ISU PAG56SG	90 ~ 110 cc

Charge Tolerance Specs

NOTES:

*Manifold Gauge Set,
Refrigerant Tank and a Scale*

Refrigerant charging. The A/C system can be properly charged either with a manifold gauge set, refrigerant tank and a scale . . .

R/R/R Machine

. . . or by using an R/R/R machine.

Always refer to the instruction manual for the equipment being used. Also make sure that the equipment is properly maintained and operating correctly.

NOTES:

FINAL A/C SYSTEM TESTS
AFTER SERVICE OR REPAIRS

Prior to returning the vehicle to the customer, the following tests should be performed to ensure proper system operation and minimize returns.

Compressor clutch voltage test. With the vehicle at normal operating temperature and the A/C system stabilized, use a digital multimeter and check voltage across the battery. Next, with the meter's negative test lead attached to the battery, back probe the compressor B+ terminal with a test pin and the positive meter lead.

Checking Voltage to the Compressor Clutch

The voltage should be within one volt of vehicle charging voltage. Next, back probe the negative terminal of the compressor clutch. The voltage should be less than 0.2 volts. If the readings deviate from these specs, further electrical circuit diagnostics must be performed.

Testing Compressor Clutch Ground Circuit Voltage Drop

NOTES:

Performance Test Gauge Readings

A/C system performance test. Refer to the vehicle manufacturer's service information and set the vehicle to the test conditions required by the manufacturer. **Always use the correct performance charts.** Compare the vehicle's A/C system performance to the charts.

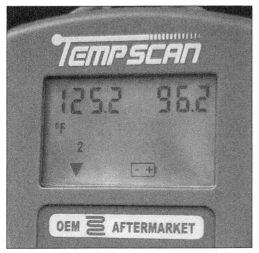

Condenser Temperature Readings

Temperature test. With the vehicle in an ambient temperature of at least 70° F, engine idling at normal operating temperature, all doors open, A/C on maximum cold, blower motor on maximum, check for the following numbers: Condenser inlet to outlet temperature difference 20-50° F. Center duct-to-ambient temperature, 30° F minimum difference. For orifice tube systems, evaporator inlet to outlet temperature ± 5° F. Temperature readings in these ranges indicate a proper charge level with no restriction in the system.

NOTES:

Leak Check. With the system fully charged and the gauge service hoses removed from the vehicle, conduct a final leak check following the SAE J1628 procedure. Check the service valves, along all lines and hoses, and pay close attention to any joints or junctions opened during repairs.

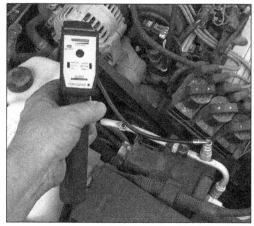

Leak Check

ALWAYS replace the port service caps – they are important.

Replace Service Caps

NOTES:

Section 9: Diagnostic Charts and Checklists

The following section contains general diagnostic routines that apply to most mobile A/C systems. The checklists are designed to cover all the components and subsystems that can affect A/C system performance and operation. These charts and checklists are guidelines only. Always check the vehicle's complete service information publications and websites for the most current and up-to-date data and specifications.

COMPRESSOR NOISE ANALYSIS

Type Of Noise	Source	Cause
Moan at specific RPM	Compressor	Groundouts
		Loose brackets/mounting bolts
		Exhaust system vibration
		Poor belt tension/tensioner Issue
Growl at idle	Compressor	Groundouts of A/C lines or components
Growl at all RPM	Compressor	Remove & check all line clamps and anchor points
Chatter at Idle	Compressor	Low refrigerant and oil charge
Whine or grind at any RPM	Compressor	Pulley bearings
	P/S Pump Generator	Interference at rotating points of pulleys Check with belt off and on
Squeal at any RPM	Compressor	Belt alignment or tension
	P/S Pump	Tensioner problems
	Generator	Belt condition
Hiss, gurgle when A/C system is turned off	Orifice Tube	Normal at shutdown isolate lines
Chirp or thump	Compressor Clutch	Occurs when A/C cycles on
Knock	Compressor	Cracked brackets/loose mounting bolts
		Drive belt tensioner faulty
		Refrigerant overcharge
		Internal compressor failure

NOTES:

PRESSURE GAUGE DIAGNOSIS

Low side	High Side	Symptoms	Diagnosis	Solutions
15 – 30 psi	110-150 psi	Poor to no cooling; compressor cycles rapidly	Low or Improper refrigerant charge	Leak check A/C system. Repair as needed. Recharge to correct level
0-15 psi or pulls into a vacuum	115-160 psi	No cooling	High side restriction or TXV stuck closed	Check temperature drop on high side lines and across condenser. Inspect TXV inlet for debris. Repair as needed
0-25 psi	150-285	Works well for awhile, airflow reduces, suction line frozen, compressor will not cycle off	Evaporator freeze up due to faulty clutch cycling switch or thermostat	Replace clutch cycling switch or thermostat
70-90 psi	90-110 psi	No cooling; compressor does not cycle off	Faulty compressor	Replace compressor
30-60 psi	350-400 psi	Poor cooling in stop and go conditions; cools during highway speeds	Refrigerant overcharge, excessive air in A/C system; condenser airflow problem	Analyze refrigerant. Recover refrigerant and recharge to correct level. Check for improper condenser airflow
	400-500 psi	Fair to poor cooling	Engine overheating; restricted airflow through condenser; cooling fan faulty	Inspect and test cooling system. Inspect and clean condenser. Check cooling fan circuit for proper operation

NOTES:

A/C SYSTEM DIAGNOSIS

Condition	Possible Cause	Repair
High and low pressures equal; compressor clutch not engaged	No refrigerant in the system	Leak test and repair system. Evacuate and recharge to the proper level
	Blown fuse	Check for proper size fuse; inspect and repair the A/C clutch circuit
	Compressor clutch coil faulty	Test clutch coil; replace as needed
	Compressor clutch relay faulty	Test the compressor clutch relay and relay circuits, repair as needed
	Compressor clutch cycling device faulty	Inspect and test the clutch cycling control. Replace as needed
	A/C pressure protection devices faulty	Inspect wiring and connectors, test devices, repair or replace as needed
	Faulty PCM/BCM	Test and replace as needed

Condition	Possible Cause	Repair
Normal operating pressure, center duct temperature too high	Excessive lubricating oil in the system	Recover refrigerant, and flush system. Restore oil to the proper level, evacuate and recharge to correct level
	Blend door faulty, out of adjustment, or not sealing	Inspect and repair the blend door as needed
	Blend door actuator faulty	Inspect, test and replace door actuator as needed

NOTES:

A/C SYSTEM DIAGNOSIS (CONTINUED)

Condition	Possible Cause	Repair
The low-side pressure is normal and the high-side pressure is too low	Low refrigerant charge	Leak test the A/C system; repair as needed. Evacuate and recharge to the correct level
	Faulty compressor	Test and replace compressor as needed

Condition	Possible Cause	Repair
System low-side pressure is normal and the high-side pressure is too high	Airflow restriction through the condenser	Inspect the condenser for bent or damaged fins, debris, or missing air dams or air seals. Clean, repair or replace as needed
	Cooling fan(s) faulty	Inspect, test and replace the cooling fan(s), inspect and repair cooling fan's circuit
	Refrigerant overcharge	Recover and recharge the A/C system to the correct level
	Excessive air in the A/C system	Analyze the refrigerant. Recover, recycle and recharge as needed
	Engine overheating	Inspect and test the cooling system, repair as needed

NOTES:

A/C SYSTEM DIAGNOSIS (CONTINUED)

Condition	Possible Causes	Repair
The low-side pressure is too high and the high-side pressure is too low	Drive belt is slipping	Inspect and replace the drive belt as needed. Inspect and test the self-tensioner, replace as needed
	Faulty expansion valve	Inspect and test the TXV; replace if necessary
	Faulty compressor	Test and replace as needed

Condition	Possible Causes	Repairs
The low-side pressure is too low and the high-side pressure is too high	Restriction in the refrigerant lines	Perform temperature test on all lines and repair or replace as needed
	Restricted refrigerant flow through the TXV	Remove and inspect the TXV, replace as needed
	Restricted refrigerant flow through the condenser	Perform temperature drop test between the condenser inlet and outlet, replace if needed

NOTES:

TEMPERATURE CHECK SHEETS

The following charts are used during A/C system temperature testing. The first set is for orifice tube systems and the next for thermostatic expansion valve.

Temperature Test for Orifice Tube Systems

Required equipment

☐ Thermocouple or a multichannel thermometer

Vehicle Setup:

☐ Ambient temperature above 70° F.

☐ Engine idling at normal operating temperature.

☐ A/C controls set at Maximum or Recirculation, Full Cold, and blower on high speed.

☐ All doors open.

☐ Connect the thermocouples to the inlet and outlet pipes of the evaporator. Be sure the probe on the inlet is past the orifice tube.

☐ Operate the A/C system for a minimum of five minutes.

Vehicle Temperature Tests:

☐ Record the evaporator inlet and outlet pipe temperatures.

☐ Move the thermocouples to the condenser inlet and outlet pipes.

☐ Record the temperature of the inlet and outlet pipes.

☐ Measure the center duct temperature of the instrument panel.

☐ Measure and record the ambient temperature.

A properly charged system will have:

☐ Evaporator inlet to outlet temperature difference of plus or minus 5° F.

☐ Condenser inlet and outlet temperature difference of 20° to 50° F.

☐ Duct temperature will be a minimum of 30° F less then ambient temperature.

If the values are not within specification, refer to the information on pages 137 through 138 for possible causes.

Orifice Tube Temperature Test Points

NOTES:

NOTES:

EVAPORATOR INLET AND OUTLET PIPES ARE THE SAME TEMPERATURE:

Charge level is correct. However, if the outlet pipe is 5° colder to 5° warmer than the inlet pipe, this is an acceptable range.

Outlet pipe is more than five degrees WARMER than inlet pipe:

System is undercharged: also check for excessive oil charge or clogged orifice tube.

Outlet pipe is more than five degrees COLDER than inlet pipe:

System is overcharged: also check for orifice tube O-ring not sealing.

Condenser

Measure the condenser inlet and outlet pipes as close to the condenser core as possible.

Inlet and outlet pipe temperature difference is 20° to 50° F:

System is correctly charged: no internal condenser restrictions.

Inlet and outlet pipe temperature difference MORE than 50° F:

System is undercharged: also check for excessive air in the system, plugged condenser internal passages.

Inlet and outlet pipe temperature difference LESS than 20° F:

System is overcharged: also check for poor airflow through condenser and radiator due to bent fins, debris, broken or missing air dams, and cooling fan problems.

AMBIENT TO CENTER DUCT TEMPERATURE:

Measure ambient air temperature at least 18 inches in front of the condenser and measure temperature in the center panel duct with the blower on high speed.

Ambient to center duct temperature difference of MORE than 30°F:

System charge is correct; evaporator is clean and blend door is closed.

Ambient to center duct temperature difference of LESS than 30°F:

Check the blend door, mode doors and heater valve (if used), faulty or out-of-adjustment. Evaporator restricted either internally: excessive oil in system, air or sealer present. Or externally: cabin filter dirty, evaporator fins plugged with debris. System possibly undercharged.

LINE AND HOSE ASSEMBLIES

Lines/hoses without mufflers: Maximum of 4° F drop from end-to-end.

Lines/hoses with mufflers: Maximum of 10° F drop from end-to-end.

NOTES:

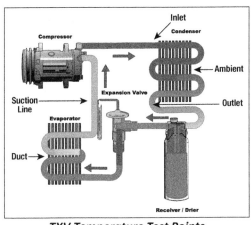

TXV Temperature Test Points

Temperature Test for TXV Systems

Required equipment

☐ Thermocouple or a multichannel thermometer

Vehicle Setup:

☐ Ambient temperature above 70° F.

☐ Engine idling at normal operating temperature.

☐ A/C controls set at Maximum or Recirculation, Full Cold, and blower on high speed.

☐ All doors open.

☐ Operate the A/C system for a minimum of five minutes.

Vehicle Temperature Tests:

☐ Connect thermocouples to the condenser inlet and outlet pipes.

☐ Record the temperature of the inlet and outlet pipes.

☐ Measure the center duct temperature of the instrument panel.

☐ Measure and record the ambient temperature.

A properly charged system will have:

☐ Condenser inlet and outlet temperature difference of 20° to 50° F.

☐ Duct temperature will be a minimum of 30° F less then ambient temperature.

If the values are not within specification, refer to the information on pages 137 through 138 for possible causes.

NOTES:

NOTES:

CHECK SHEETS

Using a diagnostic check sheet when discussing an A/C problem with the vehicle operator will ensure that the actual problem and additional problems are not overlooked.

AIR CONDITIONING & HEATING CUSTOMER QUESTIONNAIRE

CUSTOMER
Name_____ Phone_____ Date_____

Address_____ City_____ State_____ Zip_____

VEHICLE
Year_____ Make_____ Model_____ Color_____

A/C System Type – ❏ Manual ❏ Auto. Temp. Control ❏ Dual / Rear Auxiliary Unit

PROBLEM / SYMPTOM

❏	No A/C	❏	No Heat	❏	No Defrost	❏	Poor Cooling	❏	Poor Heating
❏	Improper Fan/Blower Operation	❏	Air From Wrong Outlet(s)	❏	No Temperature Control	❏	Noise Inside Car	❏	Noise Under Hood
❏	Interior Water Leak	❏	Engine Coolant Leak	❏	Warning Light(s) On	❏	Odor	❏	Other* (See Below)

WHEN DOES THE PROBLEM OCCUR?

❏	Always	❏	Intermittent	❏	When Hot	❏	When Cold	❏	At Start Up
❏	During Warm Up	❏	At Idle	❏	High Engine Speeds	❏	Driving Away From Stop	❏	At Road Speeds

Have there been any previous attempts to repair this problem? ❏ No ❏ Yes
If there were previous repair attempts, what was done? (What parts were installed, etc.)

_____

_____

Did previous repairs help the problem? ❏ No ❏ Some ❏ A lot ❏ At first, but not now.
Have repairs or service of any kind been recently performed to the vehicle? ❏ No ❏ Yes
If so, exactly what was done?

_____

_____

*FURTHER DESCRIPTION OF THE PROBLEM

_____

A/C / HEATING / VENTILATION / COOLING SYSTEM CHECKLIST

VEHICLE
Year_____ Make_____ Model_____ Engine_____

V.I.N._____ System Type – ❏ R134a ❏ R12 ❏ Retrofitted ❏ Front ❏ Rear

CUSTOMER
Name_____ Phone_____ Date_____

Address_____ City_____ State_____ Zip_____

Refrigerant I.D./Analysis - R134a_____% R12_____% Air_____% Other_____%

Gauge Readings – High Side_____psi Low Side_____psi @ _____ RPM

COMPONENT	OK	REPAIR	COMPONENT	OK	REPAIR
1. Belts			**14. Electric Cooling Fan(s)**		
Condition	❏	❏	Mounting	❏	❏
Tension	❏	❏	Operation	❏	❏
2. Belt Tensioner	❏	❏	Noise	❏	❏
3. Pulleys/Idler Pulley			Electrical Connections	❏	❏
Alignment/Spacing	❏	❏	**15. Fan Clutch**		
4. Compressor			Operation	❏	❏
Leakage	❏	❏	Fluid Leakage	❏	❏
Mounting/Alignment	❏	❏	**16. Radiator**		
Noise	❏	❏	Leakage	❏	❏
5. Compressor Clutch			Mounting	❏	❏
Air Gap	❏	❏	Cleanliness	❏	❏
Bearing	❏	❏	Hoses and Clamps	❏	❏
Field Coil	❏	❏	**17. Coolant Reservoir**	❏	❏
Electrical Connections	❏	❏	**18. Pressure Cap**	❏	❏
Surge Suppression Diode	❏	❏	**19. Thermostat**		
6. Condenser			Correct Temperature	❏	❏
Leakage	❏	❏	**20. Coolant**		
Mounting	❏	❏	Cleanliness/pH	❏	❏
Cleanliness	❏	❏	Test Results/Freeze Protection	❏	❏
7. Receiver Drier/Accumulator			**21. Heater Hoses and Clamps**	❏	❏
Mounting	❏	❏	**22. Heater Control Valve**	❏	❏
Fittings/Connections	❏	❏	**23. Evaporator**		
8. A/C Hoses and Lines			Leakage	❏	❏
Leaks	❏	❏	Connections/Fittings	❏	❏
Fittings/Connections	❏	❏	Condensate Drain	❏	❏
Rub Through	❏	❏	Odor	❏	❏
Mounting	❏	❏	**24. Panel Outlet Temperature**	❏	❏
9. Service Port Caps	❏	❏	**25. Dash Controls/Switches**		
10. Expansion Valve			Proper Air Routing	❏	❏
Leaks	❏	❏	Cable Operation	❏	❏
Sensing Bulb	❏	❏	**26. Blower Motor Operation**	❏	❏
Insulation	❏	❏	**27. A/C/Blower/Fan Relays**	❏	❏
11. Orifice Tube			**28. Underhood Switches/Controls/Sensors**		
Fittings	❏	❏	Broken	❏	❏
Leaks	❏	❏	Electrical Connections	❏	❏
12. Fan Shroud/Seals	❏	❏	Operation	❏	❏
13. Front Air Dam/Spoiler	❏	❏	Leakage	❏	❏

Section 10: Glossary

NOTES:

Air Conditioning: The process of controlling the temperature, humidity, cleanliness and distribution of the cabin air.

Accumulator: Found on orifice tube design systems, it is a liquid vapor separator that stores, filters and removes moisture from the refrigerant. It is located on the low-pressure side of the A/C system between the evaporator outlet and compressor suction side.

Ambient: Refers to the temperature surrounding a body or device under test.

Bimetal: Two metals with different rates of expansion fastened together. When heated or cooled they will warp and can be made to open or close a switch or valve.

Blower Motor: A motor driven fan used to force air through the evaporator and heater cores and circulate air through the passenger compartment.

Boiling Point: The temperature at which the addition of any heat will begin a change of state from a liquid to a vapor.

CFC or Chlorofluorocarbon: A chemical which contains chlorine, fluorine and carbon. Refrigerant 12 (R-12) is a chlorofluorocarbon.

Clutch Cycling Switch: A switch that uses the evaporator core temperature or evaporator pressure to turn the electrical circuit that controls the compressor clutch field coil off and on.

Compressor: A mechanical pump used to compress refrigerant gas and to circulate the refrigerant and oil throughout the A/C system. The three main compressor designs are: scroll, reciprocating, and rotary vane.

Compressor Clutch: An electromagnetic coupling that connects and disconnects the compressor pulley to the compressor shaft through a movable hub assembly.

Condenser: A heat exchanger usually located in front of the radiator that removes heat from the refrigerant, changing it from a hot vapor to a hot liquid.

Conduction: The transfer of heat from molecule to molecule within a substance.

Convection: The transfer of heat through a moving fluid.

Cycling Clutch Orifice Tube (CCOT): Designation for an A/C system that utilizes an accumulator and orifice tube instead of a thermostatic expansion valve and a receiver drier. This design cycles the compressor clutch on and off to prevent evaporator core freeze up.

DMM or Digital Multimeter: Electronic tester with a numerical display which is commonly used during diagnostics of electrical circuits. DMMs measure voltage and resistance, and can usually measure current and other values.

Delamination: Condition where a flexible hose's non-permeable inner barrier has separated from the hose's internal wall. This usually causes a restriction to refrigerant flow within the hose.

Discharge Line: A tube or hose that connects the compressor high-pressure side to the inlet of the condenser. The refrigerant traveling through the discharge line is high-pressure vapor.

Discharge Pressure: The pressure reading at the compressor outlet. Also called head pressure or high-side pressure.

ECM or Electronic Control Module: A microprocessor or computer that is used to control operation of an engine. An ECM receives inputs from sensors and switches, and issues output commands to devices such as fuel injectors and ignition modules.

Evaporator: A heat exchanger that removes heat from the air entering the passenger compartment. Located near the vehicle bulkhead, the refrigerant enters as a low-pressure cool, liquefied gas, and leaves as a low-pressure, cold vapor.

Freezing Point: The temperature at which a change of state from liquid to solid takes place.

HFC or Hydrofluorocarbon: A chemical which contains hydrogen, fluorine and carbon. Refrigerant 134a (R-134a) is a hydrofluorocarbon.

HFO or Hydrofluoroolefin: A type of hydrofluorocarbon. Refrigerant 1234yf (R-1234yf) is a hydrofluoroolefin.

Heat Exchanger: A device for the transfer of heat from the source to the substance to carry the heat.

Heat Flow: Heat always flows from a warmer area to a colder area. The exchange rate depends on the temperature difference, the type of materials and the size of the surrounding area.

Heat Transfer: The three methods of heat transfer are: conduction, convection, and radiation.

Latent Heat: Heat that produces a change of state without a change in temperature.

Liquid Line: The hose or tube that carries high-pressure liquid refrigerant from the condenser outlet to the refrigerant pressure control device.

Micron: A unit of measure for precise vacuum readings.

NOTES:

PAG or Polyalkylene Glycol Oil: The type of lubricating oil used in most mobile A/C systems that use R-134a refrigerant.

POE or Polyolester Oil: A type of lubricating oil used in electrically-driven compressors often found on hybrid vehicles. A different type of POE oil was required for retrofitting certain vehicles from R-12 to R-134a.

PCM or Powertrain Control Module: A microprocessor or computer that is used to control operation of an engine and other driveline components, such as transmissions and transfer cases. A PCM receives inputs from sensors and switches, and issues output commands to devices such as fuel injectors and actuators.

PWM or Pulse Width Modulation: A method used to control the operation of electrical devices, such as blower motors or solenoid-operated compressor control valves. The electricity to the device is not kept at a constant value, but rather, "pulsed" at various duty cycles. This controls the speed or rate at which the device operates.

Pressure-Temperature Relationship: The change effected in temperature when pressure is changed or the change effected in pressure when temperature is changed. An increase in temperature results in an increase in pressure. A decrease in pressure results in a decrease in temperature.

R/R/R Machine: Abbreviation for "Recovery/Recycling/Recharge" machine, a shop tool that is used to remove refrigerant from A/C systems, recycle extracted refrigerant (remove most of the moisture, oil and air that may have been present in it), and recharge A/C systems.

Radiation: The transfer of heat without use of a medium. Heat is absorbed on contact with a solid surface.

Receiver/Drier: The component used on TXV A/C system to store, filter, and absorb moisture from liquid refrigerant. It is located at the condenser or in the liquid line between the condenser outlet and the TXV inlet.

Refrigerant: The chemical substance that vaporizes and condenses to transfer heat.

Relative Humidity: The percentage of water vapor present in a given quantity of air compared to the amount it can hold at that temperature.

Sensible Heat: Heat that can be measured or felt.

Slugging: When liquid refrigerant enters the A/C compressor and creates noise and causes compressor damage.

State of Matter: Substances can exist in three states: solid, liquid, or gas.

Suction Line: The pipe or hose that carries the refrigerant vapor from the outlet of the evaporator to the inlet or suction side of the compressor.

Superheat: Additional heat added to the refrigerant vapor after the liquid refrigerant is vaporized.

System Protection Devices: Various switches and controls that prevent the compressor from operating if the A/C system pressures are too high or too low.

Temperature: The measurement of heat intensity.

Thermistor: A solid state device that varies resistance as the opposite of temperature.

Thermostat: A device that will open or close based on a change in temperature.

Thermostatic Expansion Valve: The component that controls the flow of refrigerant through the evaporator based on the superheat at the evaporator outlet.

Variable Displacement Compressor: A compressor design that uses a control valve or solenoid to adjust compressor output to match the evaporator heat load instead of cycling the compressor clutch on and off.

Vacuum: Any pressure below atmospheric pressure.

NOTES:

NOTES

NOTES

NOTES

NOTES